"Woodrow Kroll has been a frontline leader in the effort to bring back the Bible as the foundation of faith. His new book should be read by everyone who sees biblical illiteracy as a truly serious threat to the health of both religion and American society."
> —GEORGE GALLUP JR., Founder, The George H. Gallup International Institute

"Biblical illiteracy is a scandal in the church. It is high time we remedy this embarrassment and teach the Bible. I commend Dr. Kroll for raising the alarm about the lack of biblical literacy in our homes and churches."
> —R. ALBERT MOHLER JR., President, Southern Baptist Theological Seminary

"There surely is, as Amos said, a famine in our land for hearing the words of the Lord. This book is a clarion and much-needed call to combat the Bible illiteracy of our day. Dr. Kroll issues a challenge that hopefully will result in a movement to turn that famine back into a feast."
> —CHARLES CALDWELL RYRIE, author, *The Ryrie Study Bible*

"Thank God for this book that not only pinpoints a basic problem in our churches but also prescribes a cure! God has chosen Woodrow Kroll to be the man to sound the alarm of Bible illiteracy and awaken us to a vision of better days ahead!"
> —ERWIN W. LUTZER, Senior Pastor, The Moody Church, Chicago, Illinois

"It is an incredible fact that the Bible is the most sold but least read book! Dr. Kroll aims to reverse this sad statistic."
> —NORMAN L. GEISLER, Dean, Southern Evangelical Seminary

"My prayer is that God will use this book to stir you to action in overcoming Biblical illiteracy in the United States."
> —BOB CRESON, President, Wycliffe Bible Translators USA

"The doctor's diagnosis is in. The news is not good. *Taking Back the Good Book* offers an alarming analysis that will alert every Bible-believing Christian as to how we can get well. The recovery may be long, but the rehab will be worth it."
>   —MARK BAILEY, President; Professor of Bible Exposition,
>   Dallas Theological Seminary

"More than a declaration of war, this book is a battle plan for all who want to make the Bible central in their lives, their churches, and in our great nation."
>   —WARREN W. WIERSBE, author, the *Be* series

"Woodrow Kroll calls us back to our roots and challenges us to read the only book God ever wrote."
>   —KERBY ANDERSON, National Director, Probe Ministries

"Woodrow Kroll is dead-on in his assessment of the church's lack of engagement with the Word."
>   —HOWARD G. HENDRICKS, Center for Christian Leadership

HOW AMERICA FORGOT THE BIBLE
AND WHY IT MATTERS TO YOU

Taking Back the
GOOD BOOK

WOODROW KROLL

CROSSWAY BOOKS

A PUBLISHING MINISTRY OF
GOOD NEWS PUBLISHERS
WHEATON, ILLINOIS

Taking Back the Good Book: How America Forgot the Bible and Why It Matters to You

Copyright © 2007 by Woodrow Kroll

Published by Crossway Books
        a publishing ministry of Good News Publishers
        1300 Crescent Street
        Wheaton, Illinois 60187

Cover design: Josh Dennis

First printing 2007

Printed in the United States of America

ISBN-10: 1-58134-826-6

ISBN-13: 978-1-58134-826-2

Library of Congress Cataloging-in-Publication Data
Kroll, Woodrow Michael, 1944–
   Taking back the good book : how America forgot the Bible and why it matters to you / Woodrow Kroll.
      p.   cm.
   Includes bibliographical references and index.
   ISBN 13: 978-1-58134-826-2 (hc : alk. paper)
   1. United States—Church history. 2. Bible—Influence—United States.
3. Bible—United States—History. 4. Bible—Evidences, authority, etc.
5. Apologetics. I. Title.
BR515.K76   2006
2220.0973—dc22   2006026389

18	17	16	15	14	13	12	11	10	09	08	07
13	12	11	10	9	8	7	6	5	4	3	2	1

Dedicated
to
all who agree with
Martin Luther

"The Bible is alive, it speaks to me;
it has feet, it runs after me;
it has hands, it lays hold of me."

Contents

Part Five
The Impact of Bible Illiteracy
on America

Part Six
Recovering Bible Literacy
in America

Acknowledgements

The battle for Bible literacy is no mere skirmish. It's all-out war. To win this war will require many "boots on the ground"—people committed to Bible literacy and willing to stick their neck out to fight for it.

This book is not a silver bullet; it's a single shot. But like the shot heard 'round the world, I pray this single shot will start a revolution that will call America back to the Bible. Others join me in this prayer. They are the ones who have made this book possible.

Bible literacy is my passion. I have spent more than twenty-five years living and writing this book without complaint from my other passion, my wife Linda.

I want to thank those who surround me at Back to the Bible and share my passion to take back the Good Book: Arnie Cole, chief executive officer; Art Figurski, senior assistant to the president; Tami Weissert, vice president of media and communications; Mindy Kroesche, director of communications; Allen Bean, director of the Bible Literacy Development Center; and Cathy Strate, my executive assistant. There are many others.

Thanks, too, to my friends at Crossway: Lane Dennis, president; Geoff Dennis, vice president; Allan Fisher, vice president of the editorial department; Lydia Brownback, editor; Jill Carter, editorial administrator; and Sherah Baumgarten, editorial assistant.

Finally, I want to acknowledge friends like Bill Kriner, Carmen Mayell, Peter Schroeder, Warren Wiersbe, Clarence Hottel, Bryon Swanson, and dozens of pastors and others who have encouraged me to do something about Bible illiteracy in America. May this book be a beginning.

PREFACE:
Why This Book?

God placed us in one of the greatest areas of spiritual need in the entire world. Over 80 million Americans do not read the Bible or even own one.

—DAVID RAMBO

Do you remember your first Bible? I remember mine. It was red—the color; it was also read—the verb. I had a little trouble reading my first Bible because in those days I wasn't used to much more than "See Dick run. Run, Dick, run." But with time and practice, I got better at it.

There's no book like the Bible. Brides dressed in white lace often carry it on their wedding day. Soldiers carry it into battle in their shirt pockets. Presidents take the oath of office while placing their hand on it. Aging saints draw comfort from it during hours of lonely solitude. Members of the Gideons stand in pouring rain to distribute it on university campuses. Prisoners of war recite as much of it as they can from memory. None of this is true with any other book.

The Crisis Today

But the Book so many love is not the book so many read. In fact, Bible reading has declined sharply over the years. And so has Bible knowledge. What the assaults of liberal theologians couldn't do, and what the attacks of atheists couldn't do, now Satan may accomplish through a much more subtle strike.

Almost unwittingly we come to believe that the Bible is God's sacred Word, but it's simply not worth taking the time to read. What Satan could not accomplish through outside attacks, he now seeks to accomplish through simple neglect. Today, we face a real crisis: Bible illiteracy.

Our failure to understand the Bible is aiding and abetting our enemy to weaken our witness, rob us of answers to life's key questions, and keep us from enjoying the relationship with God that he made possible by revealing himself through his Word.

Now if that's not a problem to you, consider this: Bible illiteracy is stealing the next generation of Christians. We're at genuine risk of losing biblical Christianity in just one generation.

The Crisis for Our Kids

Today, 86 percent of American teenagers claim to be Christians.[1] Three out of five say they believe the Bible is totally accurate in all that it teaches.[2] These are good kids. But they are confused. They don't know the Bible for the same reason their parents don't know the Bible—neglect. Our kids want to be spiritual, but they're getting their information from all the wrong places.

Movies such as *Underworld, The Sixth Sense, The Exorcism of Emily Rose*, television programs like *Buffy the Vampire Slayer, Ghost Whisperer*, characters such as Harry Potter, books like *Goosebumps*, and even video games like *Doom* or *The Darkness* have caused our kids to buy into a spirituality that's clearly not biblical.[3]

> 73 percent of America's teens have engaged in at least one type of psychic or witchcraft-related activity.
> —*The Barna Update*, January 23, 2006

Even worse, this interest in paranormal spirituality has brought the same kids who sit in the light on Sunday morning into the darkness throughout the week. More than two million teens say they have

[1] "Teenagers' Beliefs Moving Farther From Biblical Perspectives," *The Barna Update*, October 23, 2000.
[2] Ibid.
[3] New Research Explores Teenage Views and Behavior Regarding the Supernatural," *The Barna Update*, January 23, 2006.

communicated with a dead person (10 percent). Nearly two million young people claim they have psychic powers.[4]

What our kids are getting from Christian parents and in evangelical churches is insufficient to keep them in the faith. Yes, they're frequently involved in church events and activities, but when asked if they'll continue to go to church once they're living on their own, only one out of every three teens said they will.[5] If they are the future of our churches, we're facing a crisis of biblical proportions.

Calling America Back

This book is about you, your family, and your Bible. It's about the dust on your Bible. It's about taking a reality check with regard to how deeply the plague of Bible illiteracy has wormed its way into the churches and the homes of America.

In the pages that follow we will trace the amazing impact the Bible had on the founding and formation of our country. And we'll see how a new America was born in recent decades, an America that has become hostile toward the Bible. You won't believe your eyes when you read about how close to home Bible illiteracy is. We'll also focus on the debilitating effects Bible illiteracy has on us, and how Christians are robbing themselves through simple neglect of God's Word.

Calling America back to the Bible isn't about the "good ole days." It isn't about going back to a simpler time. In fact, it's not about the past at all. It's about returning to biblical living in the future, living that is both informed and impelled by genuine Bible literacy.

We are in crisis mode. If we do nothing it could easily mean the death of any biblical expression of Christianity in the twenty-first century. We are that close. But this book is also about solutions. It's about what it will take to recover Bible literacy in America and who the key players are, including you and me. Although we've

---

[4] Ibid.
[5] "Teenagers Embrace Religion but Are Not Excited About Christianity," *The Barna Update*, January 20, 2000.

ambled a long way down the road toward Bible illiteracy, we haven't yet passed the point of no return. There are solutions and you and I are a big part of them.

> **Many people claim to have a daily routine, of which reading the Bible is just not a part. However, many feel they can change their habits if they set their mind to it.**
> **—Yankelovich marketing and advocacy study, January 13, 2006**

Thirty years ago Harold Lindsell wrote a book entitled *The Battle for the Bible*. In it he said, "A great battle rages today around biblical infallibility among evangelicals."[6] Today, the great battle isn't over Bible infallibility; it's over biblical illiteracy.

This book will both highlight the challenges presented in taking back the Book and provide a clear path to calling America back to the Bible.

---

[6] Harold Lindsell, *The Battle for the Bible* (Grand Rapids: Zondervan, 1976), preface.

1

You Can't Live without It

In all my perplexities and distresses, the Bible has never failed to give me light and strength.

—ROBERT E. LEE

There's no book like the Bible.

There's a story about an agnostic university professor visiting the island of Fiji. When he met a local chief he bemoaned the fact that missionaries had come to the island, duped the Fijian people into believing the Bible, and converted them to Christianity. Surprised, the old chief said, "See that huge rock over there? On that rock our ancestors would crush the heads of our enemies. And you see that big oven beside the rock? In that oven we would bake the bodies of our enemies before we ate them. You should be thankful for the Bible. If it weren't for that book, you'd be my lunch right now."

The Bible has changed the lives of people all over the world for millennia. It alone is a living Book, "sharper than any two-edged sword, piercing to the division of soul and of spirit, of joints and of marrow, and discerning the thoughts and intentions of the heart" (Heb. 4:12).

Throughout this book I will use a variety of adverbs to describe how to read the Bible—*consistently*, *meaningfully*, *daily*, etc. But maybe the words you're looking for are *useful*, *helpful*, and *practical*. Does it work? Is reading the Bible just something you know you should do or is it something you can't live without?

I've learned it's something I can't live without. Reading the

Bible isn't just theory; it's the key to enjoying the Christian life. It's not just an "oughta" in my life; it's a must. Let me tell you why.

Reading the Bible Prepares Us For Life

My family and I have faced our share of trials in life. Here's what I've learned that helped me prepare for them: "I have stored up your word in my heart, that I might not sin against you. Blessed are you, O LORD; teach me your statutes!" (Ps. 119:11–12). Meeting God in his Word helps me make sense out of the senselessness of life.

When the Apostle Peter wrote to his friends sprinkled throughout Asia Minor, he knew they were facing hard times. Suffering, trials, harassment, and anxiety are mentioned in each chapter of his letter (1 Pet. 1:6–7; 2:19–21; 3:17; 4:12–14; 5:6–7). So how are these Christians supposed to handle the tough times? Prepare for them.

Peter says of their trials, "Have no fear of them, nor be troubled, but in your hearts regard Christ the Lord as holy, always being prepared . . ." (1 Pet. 3:14–15). When tough times come, consider that the Lord Christ is never unholy, unfair, or unjust. Tough times come to all of us, but Jesus is always there for us when we need him.

While we all face trials in life, we don't all face them with equal confidence. The key is always to be prepared for the trials we know are coming.

> **92 percent of Americans say reading the Bible has a great deal or somewhat helped them feel at peace.**
> —*The Gallup Poll*, December 1998

But how do you do that? How do you ready yourself so when you're harassed or anxious, you don't blame God but live without fear instead? Follow the advice of the psalmist in Psalm 119: "How can a young man keep his way pure? By guarding it according to your word. With my whole heart I seek you; let me not wander from your commandments! I have stored up your word in my heart . . ." (vv. 9–11). "I will meditate on your precepts and fix my eyes on your ways. I will delight in your statutes; I will not forget your word" (vv. 15–16).

"All your commandments are sure; they persecute me with false-hood; help me! They have almost made an end of me on earth, but I have not forsaken your precepts. In your steadfast love give me life, that I may keep the testimonies of your mouth" (vv. 86–88). "Your word is a lamp to my feet and a light to my path" (v. 105).

Seek God with all your heart. Store up his Word during the good times in preparation for the bad times. Then when someone or something almost finishes you off, God's Word will light your way and give you direction and purpose not otherwise possible. Stockpiling the Bible in your life will prepare you to handle your most painful trials.

Reading the Bible Brings Peace of Mind

My father became a follower of Christ at age nineteen. God called him to ministry, and after Bible college he became a pastor. He pastored the same church for thirty-three years. He was a simple man, a hard worker, and a dedicated pastor. Some medical difficulties forced him to retire before he wanted to, but none of us knew what lay ahead.

I first noticed my father's thinking was becoming clouded in 1990. My father was to give the dedication prayer at my inauguration as the third president and Bible teacher of *Back to the Bible*. He was a bit at loose ends in his remarks before offering the prayer, but I thought he was just nervous. In subsequent years his mental confusion became more noticeable. Finally he was diagnosed with Alzheimer's.

"The long goodbye," as Alzheimer's is called, is a difficult trauma for the whole family. My father suffered from Alzheimer's for thirteen years, and our whole family suffered too. In his last years, he was a resident in a geriatric Alzheimer's facility in Virginia. His physical condition deteriorated steadily but watching his mental deterioration was the most disheartening. When my wife, Linda, and I visited, he didn't know who we were. He couldn't speak. His stare pierced right through us.

Although my father never appeared to be *there* on our visits, we would never leave without singing a hymn and reading some Scripture. That's when the most amazing thing happened. As I read a familiar passage to him, my father would mouth the words. It was amazing. We were never sure how much cognitive function he had, but when he heard the Word, what he had stored up for years would flow over his lips. The Bible never loses its power to bring peace to the mind.

Reading the Bible Brings Comfort to the Soul

I have been very blessed in my life. I became a Christian at age five. I grew up in a wonderful Christian family. I met and married the girl of my dreams. We have four godly children and fourteen grandchildren. I have been privileged to serve the Lord through some incredible ministries. I have the opportunity to teach the Word of God daily to millions all around the world.

But there have been tough times too. Sometimes, even when you believe you are following the leading of the Lord, you find yourself in situations that shake you to the core of your being.

> Research indicates that people do not pray for God to reveal truth to them.
> —The Bible Literacy Center, May 18, 2006

At one point in my life, I became disillusioned in a ministry position. I was deeply discouraged. I had a valuable ministry, but I knew something was wrong. I knew I was in the wrong place of service. I told the Lord, "I'll do anything, and I'll go anywhere—just give me a clue." Have you been there?

Nothing. I prayed and asked him to make his way plain. He was silent. I wasn't willing to just jump ship; I wanted to know I was doing what God wanted me to do. But I just didn't know what that was.

Many times in the evening I would sit alone with my Bible in my lap. I would read awhile, and pray awhile. Then I would just sit, wait, and repeat the cycle again. What I needed, I thought, was guidance. But what I got was an intimacy with God that prepared me for ministry the rest of my life.

During those dark days of confusion, frustration, and bewilderment, the only comfort I received was the comfort of God's Word. Just when I was at the lowest point of my life, God would bring some truth to my thoughts that would lift my spirits and keep me going another day.

More than two years later my long nightmare was over. God brought his will right to my doorstep, and I have never looked back. But I learned a very valuable lesson during those nights of reading my Bible and praying: when you want the God of all comfort by your side, you have to know where to find him. I found him each evening in his Word, and that sustained me.

Reading the Bible Provides Strength for Your Journey

When you're consistent in reading the Bible and making its truths your own, it's always there when you need it, and you never know when that will be.

Our children gave Linda and me five beautiful granddaughters. Then five handsome, little grandsons. Then the tie breaker, a girl, and the evener, a boy, another girl to break the tie, and now another boy. It's our first "evener" who has taught me valuable lessons about the personal benefit of storing up the Bible for unexpected challenges.

The evener is Thaddeus Leighton Percival. Thaddeus was born with Treacher Collins Syndrome, a cranial-facial genetic disorder that affects the head and face.[1] When our daughter Tiffany was carrying Thaddeus (she has two older sons and now a younger daughter), we knew something was wrong. The doctors advised us to be

[1] To learn more about Treacher Collins Syndrome, contact The National Craniofacial Association, P. O. Box 11082, Chattanooga, TN 37401 or www.faces-cranio.org/Disord/Treacher.htm.

prepared for a condition called Pierre Robbin Syndrome which also affects the jaw and face. We immediately became Internet experts and said to ourselves, "We can handle this."

On the day that Thaddeus was born, Linda and I were in Bermuda at a Bible conference. We anxiously awaited a call, and when it finally came I inquired how our daughter weathered the delivery. She was fine. Then I asked, "Tell me about Thaddeus." Tiffany said, "It's worse than we thought." She then told me to sit down.

"He has no ears," she said. I remember how numb my mind was when I heard those words. "What do you mean he has no ears?" I questioned. "He has no ear at all, on either side of his head, and there's no opening for the ear canal. He has two tiny ear lobes but no external ear." But there was more.

Because of his cranial-facial deformity, the doctors had to do a tracheostomy on our newborn Thaddeus. He breathes only through his trach. And because his chin is set against the back of his throat, he cannot eat or swallow. We feed him every day through a stomach tube.

Thaddeus is now four years old. He's had multiple surgeries, and we're now awaiting a major surgery where the team of doctors will roll back the skin of his face, take marrow from his ribs, and form some of the facial bones that he's been missing from birth.

But don't pity us. Thaddeus is a great joy in our lives. And don't pity Thaddeus. He's a happy little guy who apparently doesn't know anything is wrong with him. I don't tell you all of this so that you'll feel sorry for us. I'm telling you this story to encourage you, because it certainly has encouraged me.

When Tiffany called us the night Thad was born, after she described him to me, she began to cry. Through her sobs she managed to ask, "Daddy, what do we do now?" I responded instinctively from my heart, but now that I think back on my answer it came from the strength of knowing God's Word. When she asked what we do now I said, "Tiffany, today is the day we live the faith we've talked about all these years."

> **We will not believe more than we know, and we will not live higher than our beliefs.**
> —R. Albert Mohler Jr.

Saying that the Bible brings strength for the journey is only theory until it's your journey that hits some rough spots. When we returned to Nebraska and went to the hospital to see our new, little grandson, I was able to hold him in my arms even with all the tubes and monitors. As I looked into his beautiful but different face, I knew nothing could rob us of the joy of loving him. It would be those daily portions of God's Word that we had fed on for years that would sustain us now.

Ultimately we read the Bible because it is the only Book God ever wrote, and we dishonor him when we fail to read it. But on the practical side, we read the Bible because we need the Bible. It's the only book that brings sanity to the insanity of a sinful world.

The Bible helps make sense in my life when the world doesn't. When you fail to read the Bible, you rob God of the honor of being the Author of a well-read book. But you also rob yourself of peace, comfort, strength, and a sense that God will make all things right. If you ask me, that's a price too high to pay.

2

Reasons to Read
the Bible

It's not a matter of memorizing information, it's a matter of knowing God. As we know Him and are intimate with Him, then the information we have about Him is going to be an indicator of what our level is with Him.

—BARRY SHAFER

Do you need a reason to read your Bible? Maybe in your heart you said *no*, but what about in your head? Did you say *probably*? Let's face it. Maybe one of the reasons people don't read the Bible today is that they can't think of a good reason to do so.

For me, reading my Bible is not about duty. Oh sure, I feel keenly that since God only wrote one Book, he'd be pleased to have us read it. But obligation is not enough reason for most people to read the Bible. So, let's think in other terms. What will we miss if we don't read the Bible?

When we fail to read the Word we rob ourselves. We are the poorer for not knowing what the Bible says. But what are some concrete reasons why we should read the Bible, things that make a difference in our everyday lives? Well, in the style of David Letterman on *The Late Show*, here are my "Top Ten" reasons to read the Bible. Maybe some of them will be your reasons too.

Reason 10: Reading the Bible Gives You Confidence

When your friends and family are struggling emotionally, when they seem to be at sea spiritually, who do they come to looking for answers? Is it you? And if they do, why is that?

One of the great benefits of reading the Bible is discovering God's answers to life's issues. If you've read your Bible in a meaningful way, you can confidently help your friends and family who are still searching. The answers they still seek you have already discovered in the Bible. You become the *go-to* guy or gal in your family or circle of friends.

When the last king of Judah, Zedekiah, was trying to hold onto his kingdom in the chaos just before the Babylonian captivity, he asked the prophet Jeremiah, "Is there any word from the LORD?" Jeremiah replied, "There is" (Jer. 37:17). That's the kind of confidence you need.

> **85 percent of people surveyed say reading the Bible is very important to them.**
> —The Bible Literacy Center, May 18, 2006

After your friends have tried their New Age unreality and are left with a whole lot of emptiness, after they've become fed up with organized religion and are still searching for real answers, they're going to need someone to speak confidently to them about the realities of life. That's when you need the confidence that consistent Bible reading brings. "In quietness and confidence shall be your strength" (Isa. 30:15 NKJV).

Reason 9: Reading Your Bible Insulates You Against Satan's Attacks

Failure to read and study God's Word is an open invitation to the devil. It's a way of waving a red flag in his face and saying, *Come get me. I'll fall for anything.*

Syndicated columnist Cal Thomas wrote, "While I was working as a reporter for a Houston television station in the 1970s, I interviewed Madalyn Murray O'Hair, the atheist 'credited' with the lawsuit that led the Supreme Court to declare organized prayer and Bible reading in public schools unconstitutional. I asked Mrs. O'Hair why so many people were afraid of her. I will never forget her reply: 'I'll tell you, Mr. Thomas, why some Christians are afraid of me.

They're not sure that what they believe is really true. If they were sure, I wouldn't be a threat to them at all.'"[1]

Jesus said, "You will know the truth, and the truth will set you free" (John 8:32). Free from what? Look at what Jesus said. Since he would be leaving the world to rejoin the Father while his disciples would be staying in the world, the disciples needed to be preserved from the world's evils. Jesus prayed to his Father and requested that the disciples be sanctified (set apart to be more like him) from the world and from the evil one by their knowledge of the truth found in God's Word (17:17).

By reading your Bible consistently and meaningfully, you put on God's armor and that helps you defend yourself when Satan attacks you (Eph. 6:10–18). When you fail to read your Bible, Satan will take advantage of it. He loves an unarmed enemy!

Reason 8: Reading Your Bible Helps You Think Christianly

Harry Blamires begins his extraordinary book, *The Christian Mind*, with this amazing statement: "There is no Christian mind. . . . As a thinking being," he writes, "the modern Christian has succumbed to secularization. He accepts religion—its morality, its worship; but he rejects the religious view of life, the view which sets all earthly issues within the context of the eternal."[2]

Blamires is saying that twenty-first-century Christians have become so biblically ignorant they have forfeited any chance of thinking Christianly. Christians accept the idea of living a moral life and worshiping God in church, but nothing in their lives is so transformed that the neighbors notice the difference or the boss wonders what's happened to them. They don't view the world any differently than nonbelievers.

But we can change that. As we consistently read and practice God's Word, the Spirit of God teaches us how to think as God thinks (John 14:26; 1 Cor. 2:10–12). Paul says that's how we "have the

---

[1] Cal Thomas and Ed Dobson, *Blinded by Might* (Grand Rapids: Zondervan, 1999), 92.
[2] Harry Blamires, *The Christian Mind: How Should a Christian Think* (London: SPCK, 1963), 3–4.

mind of Christ" (1 Cor. 2:16). God reveals his mind through his Son, Jesus, and through his Word, the Bible. When we read God's Word and then do what we read, we reflect the mind of Christ and think like him.

So immerse your mind in the mind of Christ through God's Word and you won't give in to secular thinking. Think differently. Don't just ask *what would Jesus do?* Ask *how would Jesus think?*

Reason 7: Reading Your Bible Helps You Define Morality

We've been told for decades that we cannot legislate morality. The evangelical community has been hammered for holding views that run counter to the culture of the day. Often we've been silent simply because the postmodern world has been so vocal. We've been squeezed into the world's mold that defines morality in terms of societal acceptability (Rom. 12:1–2).

> **89 percent of Americans say reading the Bible has a great deal or somewhat 'strengthened me to stand up against wrongs in society.'**
> —*The Gallup Poll*, December 1998

A few years ago a football coach for the Nebraska Cornhuskers was the guest on a talk show on a Christian radio station. He said Christians need to show love for homosexuals the way Christ loves people, but we must not endorse their sinful lifestyle. Well, you would have thought the coach was a flaming homophobic bigot. Everyone jumped on him. A local cantor at the Jewish synagogue said that was the kind of talk that led to the death of Matthew Shepard (a Wyoming student who was sinfully bludgeoned to death because he was a homosexual). A university English professor, who happened to be the co-chair of the Committee on Gay, Lesbian, Bisexual and Transgender Concerns, called the coach's statements terribly misguided.

And what did the Christian community have to say? Virtually nothing. But think about this—if we as Christians read our Bibles more, we'd be better able to define biblical morality and make a deeper impact in the public arena.

Reason 6: Reading Your Bible Enables You to Discover Hope

Woody Allen, though a comedian by profession, spoke for so many people when he said, "More than at any other time in history, mankind faces a crossroads. One path leads to despair and utter hopelessness. The other, to total extinction. Let us pray that we shall have the wisdom to choose correctly. I speak, by the way, not with any sense of futility, but with a panicky conviction of the absolute meaninglessness of existence."[3]

So many people live with a belief that there's no existence beyond the grave and therefore there's nothing to live for. They see the world as meaningless. They believe God is dead, or at least so distant he has no interest in them. They're devoid of hope. They don't know where to turn, so they have turned inward to themselves. There, too, they've found only disappointment.

Contrast that with the message of the Bible. Paul describes the Gentiles as being "separated from Christ, alienated from the commonwealth of Israel and strangers to the covenants of promise, having no hope and without God in the world" (Eph. 2:12). That's a pretty dismal picture. But the apostle continues, "But now in Christ Jesus you who once were far off have been brought near by the blood of Christ. For he himself is our peace" (vv. 13–14).

Only the Bible can offer the world what it really needs in an era of meaninglessness. And when you read your Bible, you not only gain hope but you have hope to share with your hopeless friends and family.

Reason 5: Reading Your Bible Identifies the "Center" in Your Life

Have you ever used a level to hang a picture or to make sure a wallpaper border was the same distance from the floor all around the

---

[3] Woody Allen, "Adrift Alone in the Cosmos," *New York Times*, August 10, 1979.

room? The secret is the bubble; when the bubble is in the center, all is right with the world.

The Bible has always been our *bubble* bringing us back to the center where we remember things that are right. However, with growing Bible illiteracy, the center today is all over the room. Historian David Wells appropriately issues this warning to the twenty-first-century church:

> Despite the earlier prophecies that as the culture became more secularized, religion would vanish, polls now show that substantial belief is still intact. . . . The question, of course, is what all of this means, for while all of the elements of a traditional Christian faith are apparently surviving modernity, American life is nevertheless being redefined by modernity in such a way that the United States is no longer evidently a Christian country, no matter how loosely the word Christian is used. What, then, is the place of this belief in the modern mind? Is it at the center, or is it on the periphery? Does it define who a person is, or must that definition be sought elsewhere?[4]

If we allow postmodern society to identify what is Christian, what is right, what is just, rather than the Bible, we'll be as much at sea as the world around us. It's the Bible that keeps our bubble in the center.

Reason 4: Reading Your Bible Helps You Discover Who You Are

Many people believe that what they can do defines who they are. Who is the basketball star when he or she can no longer run up and down the court? Most athletes don't know.

Others define who they are in terms of their job. Interesting, isn't it, that when we meet someone for the first time, after asking their name we always ask, "What do you do for a living?" Presumably what we do defines our worth and gives us identity. That would

[4]David F. Wells, *No Place for Truth* (Grand Rapids: Eerdmans, 1993), 106–7.

mean a brain surgeon is more valuable than a plumber, unless, of course, you have a leaky pipe.

The Bible defines our identity much differently. It says we were created by God with significance. We were the capstone of his creation, the last thing he created (Gen. 1:23–27). We were created directly by God's hand rather than by the usual method of speaking things into existence. God breathed the breath of life into us; he didn't do that for anything else in his creation (Gen. 2:7). We were created in his image, after his likeness (Gen. 1:26). Nothing else in creation was so made.

The Bible says we're very special to God. And yet we severed that special relationship with sin. We lost our significance because it existed only in our special relationship with God. But read on in your Bible. It tells us how to regain that special relationship through Jesus Christ and in doing so to regain our significance. A fantastic benefit to reading your Bible is to discover who you are "in Christ Jesus." Once you do, you'll never live the same way again.

Reason 3: Reading Your Bible Guides You to Intimacy with God

Early in Moses' leadership, God did a very special thing for him. He called Moses and Aaron, Nadab and Abihu, and the seventy elders of Israel near the top of Mount Sinai to worship him (Ex. 24:1). Then in verse 2 we see that God did something extraordinary for Moses. He called Moses to step forward alone and come closer to God—nobody else; just Moses.

> **93 percent of Americans say reading the Bible has a great deal or somewhat helped them feel closer to God.**
> —*The Gallup Poll,* December 1998

You probably won't get an engraved invitation from God, but you can experience something extraordinary. By reading your Bible consistently, you can become more intimate with God. He will quench your spiritual thirst (Ps. 42:1) and speak to you in the soft whisper of someone close to you (1 Kings 19:12). You can say with the psalmist, "My soul thirsts for God, for the living God. When shall I come and appear before God?" (Ps. 42:2).

Do you want to get to know God better? Do you want to live in a dynamic relationship with him? Then keep your appointment with him and benefit from meeting him every day in the pages of his Word. Claim his promise: "You keep him in perfect peace whose mind is stayed on you" (Isa. 26:3). Put your mind in the right place. Read God's Word faithfully and live in perfect peace and intimacy with your heavenly Father.

Reason 2: Reading Your Bible Helps Make You Special

Everybody wants to be special, to stand out in some way. God wants you to stand out for him. But that won't happen unless you're familiar with his Word. What the Apostle Paul wrote in Titus 2:14 doesn't get a lot of press because it comes on the heels of that great verse about the blessed hope. But 2:14 is every bit as important as 2:13 because it tells us the two reasons why Jesus died for us: "[He] gave himself for us to redeem us from all lawlessness and to purify for himself a people for his own possession who are zealous for good works."

Most of us know that Jesus died to redeem us from the marketplace of sin, but did you know he also died to purify you and make you the kind of person who stands out from the world? Today we have a lot of "barcode Christians." They are all alike. Swipe their barcode, and they'll be like every other Christian. They sing the same praise choruses, listen to the same Christian artists, dress the same, think the same, and act the same. They are exactly what the world's barcode says they should be. Nobody is different; nobody stands out.

The reason why many Christians today are just like everyone else is they don't know what makes the Christian life distinctive. They haven't read enough of God's Word to know the importance of being special to God, zealous to do the right thing, and live for God's glory.

> **52 percent of respondents said they usually get something useful from reading the Bible.**
> —Yankelovich marketing and advocacy study, January 13, 2006

If you've had it with being a barcode Christian, read your Bible and become something else. Become a special person to God, cleansed from habitual sin and serving him in a way that makes you stand out.

Reason 1: Reading Your Bible Helps You Change Your World

I took my earphones off, slid back in my chair, and crossed my legs behind a table in a radio studio in Sydney. Across from me was the station manager of the largest Christian radio station in Australia. We had just finished a thirty-minute live interview, and now we were just going to talk. We chatted about how to work together to win Australia for Christ, but it was immediately evident our approaches were worlds apart. My approach was to teach the Word to a thirsty world; his approach was to sneak up on sinners.

Many Christians, including this radio station manager, practice "pre-evangelism." Unlike a clear presentation of God's provision for man's need, pre-evangelism softens up the world by building bridges to the unsaved. In the case of this station, they played almost nothing but rock music and every so often they would include a song that mentioned God. To my Aussie friend, this was pre-evangelism. When I asked him what percentage of their programming was distinctively Christian he replied, "Fourteen percent," and then he gleefully added, "Most Christians don't even know this is a Christian station."

My deluded colleague apparently hadn't read enough of God's Word to understand the patterns of New Testament evangelism. Pre-evangelism is fine, as long as it leads to evangelism. But when the message is never shared, pre-evangelism is no better than no evangelism at all.

Do you want to change your world? There is only one thing

powerful enough to do that, and that's the gospel—the good news that Jesus Christ died for our sins. "It is the power of God for salvation" (Rom. 1:16). The Bible changes the world, unlike sneaking in a song that merely mentions God. Reading your Bible and living out what it says will help you change your world. After all, "Faith *comes* by hearing, and hearing by the word of God" (Rom. 10:17 NKJV). There is no other way, just the Bible way.

The benefits to reading your Bible are only appreciated as they are experienced. Isn't it time we stopped robbing ourselves of all that God has for us? Isn't it time we all got back to the Bible?

Part Two

The Bible's Historic Influence on America

The Bible did not just give impetus to the founding and formation of America; it was the basis of that founding and formation.
—WOODROW KROLL

3

The Bible and America's Beginnings

It is impossible to enslave mentally or socially a Bible-reading people. The principles of the Bible are the groundwork of human freedom.

—HORACE GREELEY

I was born in the United States of America. To some, that makes me evil; to others, it makes me lucky. To me, it makes me an American. I'm proud of my country. It's not perfect, but as an American, I still get shivers up my spine when someone sings "America the Beautiful." Perhaps the most meaningful phrase in the song is, "America! America! God shed his grace on thee."[1]

I've been privileged to visit and preach God's Word in more than one hundred countries of the world, and I'm convinced that no nation on earth has been blessed by God's grace as has America. I also believe a great deal of that divine blessing is due to America's biblical roots and infancy.

Bringing Faith to the New World

America had the good fortune to be founded by people who strongly believed the Bible. When these pioneers arrived in this new land, the influence of the Bible on their literature, their music, and their

---

[1] Katharine Lee Bates, *America the Beautiful*. Falmouth Historical Society. Katharine Lee Bates wrote the original version in 1893. She wrote the second version in 1904. Her final version was written in 1913. Here is a note from Katharine Lee Bates: "One day some of the other teachers and I decided to go on a trip to 14,000-foot Pikes Peak. We hired a prairie wagon. Near the top we had to leave the wagon and go the rest of the way on mules. I was very tired. But when I saw the view, I felt great joy. All the wonder of America seemed displayed there, with the sea-like expanse."

lives came with them. Their Christian faith was as much a part of who they were as their bold spirit.

The first book printed in the Colonies was *The Bay Psalm Book*—a book of psalms to be sung. There was no need immediately to publish Bibles in the New World; these deeply religious people brought their Bibles with them.[2]

The influence of the Bible and the Christian religion was very much in evidence in the New England colonies and in other colonies as well. The New Jersey, Pennsylvania, and Maryland colonies considered themselves to be "plantations of religion." Most of the charters mention the desire of the stockholders to convert the natives and to extend Christ's dominion.[3]

While some of the early settlers of America came for commercial reasons, the great majority left Europe and England to worship God as their consciences interpreted the Bible. Thus, they enthusiastically supported the efforts of their leaders to use settlement in the New World as a "holy experiment," to create "a city on a hill."[4] They believed their success was part of God's plan to evangelize the world. Even in colonies like Virginia, which were largely commercial ventures, the settlers considered themselves "militant Protestants" and worked tirelessly to establish the church in the New World and teach the Bible to those already living here.

The influence of the Bible on the earliest days of the American experiment was enormous. It was the early Americans' guide, their rule of life, their comfort during hardship, and their hope for the

---

[2] Neil Postman, *Amusing Ourselves to Death* (New York: Penguin, 1985), 31.

[3] Peter G. Mode, *Source Book and Bibliographical Guide for American Church History* (Menasha, WI: George Banta Publishing, 1921), 9–10, 26.

[4] William Bradford, the first governor of the Plymouth Bay Colony. In chapter 9 of Bradford's personal history of the first several years of the colony, the governor imagined the children of the original Pilgrims making this confession: "Our faithers were Englishmen which came over this great ocean, and were ready to perish in this wildernes; but they cried unto the Lord, and he heard their voyce, and looked on their adversitie, etc. Let them therfore praise the Lord, because he is good, and his mercies endure for ever. Yea, let them which have been redeemed of the Lord, shew how he has delivered them from the hand of the oppressour. When they wandered in the deserte wildernes out of the way, and found no citie to dwell in, both hungrie, and thirstie, their sowle was overwhelmed in them. Let them confess before the Lord his loving kindness, and his wonderfull works before the sons of men. (William Bradford, "Of Plimouth Plantation," in *The Literature of the United States* (Chicago: Scott, Foresman and Company, 1957), 32.

future. It was also a reflection of the times. Just twenty-five years after the "discovery" of America, a monk named Martin Luther tacked his ninety-five theses to the church door in Wittenberg, and living by biblical truth became a passion for many. That's the spirit these brave settlers brought to America.

The role of the Bible and religion in the founding of our country is clear. The record is there in black and white. Every evidence indicates the profound effect God's Word had on early Americans. Our nation has deep roots in the Word of God.

The Bible's Influence on Old America's Government

Those who established the government of Old America, the America of our nation's infancy and growth, were equally people who trusted God's Word and looked to it for guidance. So influential was the Bible in the formation of early American political thought and governance that hardly any of America's founding fathers were silent on the importance of the Bible. President George Washington (1789–1797), America's first military and political leader, said, "It is impossible to rightly govern the world without God and the Bible."[5]

> So great is my veneration of the Bible . . . I have for many years made it a practice to read through the Bible once every year.
>
> —John Quincy Adams

Andrew Jackson, the seventh United States president (1829–1837), said, "Go to the Scriptures . . . the joyful promises it contains will be a balsam to all your troubles. That book . . . is the rock on which our republic rests."[6] The first seven United States presidents—George Washington, John Adams, Thomas Jefferson, James Madison, James Monroe, John Quincy Adams, and Andrew Jackson—all made

[5] www.earstohear.net/Heritage/quotes.html.
[6] Ibid.

strong statements recognizing the importance of the Bible in governing our nation.

The Bible also had tremendous impact on other heroes who helped to shape America, including Benjamin Franklin, John Witherspoon, and Noah Webster. Ben Franklin was the only person to sign all four of the critical documents marking the birth of America as a nation. Witherspoon was both powerful preacher and president of Princeton University, an institution that fanned America's flame of freedom. And Noah Webster created our country's first dictionary with American spellings and pronunciations.[7]

But the Bible didn't merely influence the thinking of the men God used to shape the American dream; it dictated it. The Bible was basic to Old American leaders' concept of government. They read it frequently, quoted it freely, and expressed their faith in print. And the documents they produced reveal an underlying debt to the Bible.

The Declaration of Independence

The premier of these documents, the Declaration of Independence, begins with these words:

> When in the Course of human events, it becomes necessary for one people to dissolve the political bands which have connected them with another, and to assume among the powers of the earth, the separate and equal station to which the Laws of Nature and of Nature's God entitle them, a decent respect to the opinions of mankind requires that they should declare the causes which impel them to the separation. We hold these truths to be self-evident, that all men are created equal, that they are endowed by their Creator

---

[7] Benjamin Franklin signed the Declaration of Independence, the treaty with France, the peace agreement with England, and the Constitution of the United States. Franklin said, "A Bible and a newspaper in every house, a good school in every district—all studied and appreciated as they merit—are the principal support of virtue, morality, and civil liberty." John Witherspoon was a true evangelical who represented New Jersey at the Continental Congress and signed the Declaration of Independence. For Witherspoon, religious faith was essential in fostering true liberty. And Noah Webster, himself a strong man of faith, said, "All the miseries and evils which men suffer from vice, crime, ambition, injustice, oppression, slavery and war, proceed from their despising or neglecting the precepts contained in the Bible." America's lexicographer made his own translation of the Bible in 1833.

with certain unalienable Rights, that among these are Life, Liberty and the pursuit of Happiness.[8]

These exalted words clearly demonstrate the firm belief our American forefathers had in God and his Word. David Barton claims "almost half of the signers of the Declaration (24 of 56) held what today would be considered seminary or Bible school degrees."[9] Of the fifty-six signers of the Declaration of Independence, all but two or three were Christians who read their Bible consistently and lived in light of what they read.

> 34 percent of the contents of America's founding documents were direct quotations from the Bible.
> —National Council on Bible Curriculum in Public Schools

A Nation of Faith

Belief in God and his Word is also evident in other areas of our country's history. Here are a few examples. The idea of three branches of government, proposed by James Madison at the Constitutional Convention of 1787, was strongly influenced by Isaiah 33:22: "For the LORD is our judge; the LORD is our lawgiver; the LORD is our king; he will save us." The presidential oath of office includes several religious elements, added by George Washington, including placing the hand on the Bible and the words, "So help me God!" at the end of the oath.

The Liberty Bell is inscribed with the words: "Proclaim liberty throughout the land and to all the inhabitants thereof." This is a direct quote from Leviticus 25:10. The Great Seal of the United States of America features a depiction of "Moses lifting his wand and dividing the Red Sea." Government and public buildings often feature verses from the Bible. "In God We Trust" is prominently displayed above the Speaker's rostrum in the House of Representatives.

---

[8] If you would like to secure copies of America's founding documents such as the Declaration of Independence, the Bill of Rights, or the Mayflower Compact, contact: Wallbuilders at wbcustomerservice@wallbuilders.com.

[9] David Barton, "God: Missing in Action from American History," *NRB Magazine*, June 2005.

The east pediment outside the United States Supreme Court contains the figure of Moses holding tablets of the laws of God. A marble relief portrait of Moses directly faces the speaker from the back of the House of Representatives. And the words, "Praise be to God" can be found in the cap of the Washington Monument.

State and local governments of America were also influenced by the words of Scripture. All you need to do is read your state constitution and you will see the powerful biblical influence on Old America.[10]

- The Declaration of independence refers to God four times.
- *The Star-Spangled Banner* and the Pledge of Allegiance also include the name of God.
- There is a prayer room in the United States Capitol building that includes a stained-glass window of George Washington praying.
- In 1800 Congress approved having church services in the Capitol.
- 94 percent of America's founding documents were based on the Bible.
- Our national motto is "In God We Trust."

The people who founded the United States of America were strong advocates of God's Word. They read their Bibles. They believed them. They cherished them. They lived by them. That created an America that, if not Bible-guided, was at least Bible-friendly. It was an America whose people believed with all their hearts: "America! America! God shed his grace on thee."

---

[10] Three examples: (1) North Carolina, 1776, Article IV, Section 2: "The thirty-second of the Constitution shall be amended as follows: No person who shall deny the being of God, or the truth of the Christian religion, or the Divine authority of the Old or New Testaments, or who shall hold principles incompatible with the freedom and safety of the state, shall be capable of holding any office, or place of trust or profit, in the civil department within this State." 2) Vermont, 1793, Chapter I, Article 3: "That all men have natural and unalienable rights to worship Almighty God according to the dictates of their own consciences and understandings, as in their opinion shall be regulated by the Word of God." 3) Tennessee 1834, Article IX, Section 2: "No person who denies the being of God, or a future state of rewards and punishment, shall hold any office in the civil department of this State."

4

The Bible and America's Education and Culture

Education is useless without the Bible.

—NOAH WEBSTER

How well I remember those cold mornings when my mother would wake my brother and me, dress us in front of the open kitchen stove door, and send us down the road to catch the school bus. Once we got to school and found our seats, the first order of business was to read the Bible, say the Pledge of Allegiance to the American flag, and recite the Lord's Prayer.

The Bible may not have been an official part of the curriculum, but it was a part of our lives. This was the way it was when I went to public school and it was done that way long before you and I were old enough to go to school.

The Bible's Influence on Old America's Education

Apart from the family, no institution has a greater influence on shaping society than education. Schools in America were originally a support system for the family. They reinforced the values and beliefs of the family, values and beliefs which were rooted in the Bible. As writer Stephen Bates notes, public education in America began as "an intrinsically religious undertaking."[1]

The religious beliefs of America's earliest settlers were reflected in the education of their children. For more than a century, American

---

[1] Stephen Bates, *Battleground: One Mother's Crusade, the Religious Right, and the Struggle for Control of Our Classrooms* (New York: Poseidon Press, 1993), 40.

youngsters learned to read from *The New England Primer*.[2] First published in 1690, this little book taught the alphabet with rhyming couplets based on biblical events and by using two-line "lessons for youth" reflecting the Puritan understanding of the Bible.[3]

> **How glorious is our heavenly King, Who reigns above the Sky,**
>
> **How shall a child presume to sing His dreadful Majesty?**
> —The first words of *The New England Primer*

The New England Primer taught children how to read, write, and speak the English language. And unashamedly at the same time, it taught them moral and ethical values taken directly from the Bible.

After the American Revolution, Noah Webster's famous speller, *The American Spelling Book*, replaced *The New England Primer* as the most widely used beginner reading book in schools, but the influence of the Bible remained. While the purpose of his book was to establish a common English language for the new nation, Webster included instructional passages and stories with a strong religious tenor to them. Webster believed that "The Bible was America's basic textbook in all fields." As a result, Webster's speller contained phrases like, "No man may put off the law of God. My joy is in His law all the day."[4]

The greatest textbook series of all time, *McGuffey's Readers*, had a significant influence on American education. The most popular textbooks of the nineteenth century, *McGuffey's Readers* were thoroughly biblical in their lessons. McGuffey often wrote stories that taught biblical morality and lifted principles straight from the Bible that everyone recognized as coming from the pages of Holy Scripture.[5]

---

[2] All quotes are from the original *The New England Primer* (Boston: Edward Draper, 1777). Reprint, The Vision Forum, Inc. (San Antonio, TX: 2004).

[3] As an example, consider the first six letters of the alphabet: A—In Adam's fall we sinned all; B—Heaven to find, the Bible mind; C—Christ crucified for sinners died; D—The Deluge drowned the Earth around; E—Elijah hid by ravens fed; F—the judgment made Felix afraid.

[4] Noah Webster, *The American Spelling Book* (Wilmington, DE: Bonsal & Niles, 1800).

[5] William H. McGuffey, *The Eclectic First Reader, for Young Children.* (Milford, MI: Mott Media, Inc., 1982), 56–59. Lesson XX of McGuffey's *The Eclectic First Reader* says: "John Jones was a good boy, but he could not read nor write. His mother was poor. She could not

In fact, one-third of the readers used in public schools in 1837 contained religious teaching.[6]

> **Cursed be all learning that is not subservient to the cross of Christ.**
>
> —Jonathan Witherspoon

Early American education used the Bible for instruction and its teachings were firmly rooted in God's Word. The Bible's influence on education in the early generations of American history was significant, it was desirable, and it was unquestioned.

The Bible's Influence on Old America's Culture

The Bible influenced America's founding, our early government, our leaders, and the origins of American public education. But the Bible also had a major impact on everyday life. Over the years the names Americans have given their children have often been Bible names. Names like John, Mary, Jeremiah, Abigail, Josiah, Peter, Sarah, Paul, and Elizabeth have been widely popular. That trend

---

pay for him to go to school. She sent him out to help a man at the side of the road to break stones. John could not earn much, it is true, yet it was good for him to be at work. It is well for us all to have work to do. It is bad for us not to work. John was a good boy, and he did not love to play so much that he could not work. He knew it to be right to work, and when his work was done he would play. The man for whom John worked was very kind to John, and gave him a great deal of good advice. One day he said to him, 'John, you must always bear in mind, that it was God who made you, and who gave you all that you have, and all that you hope for. He gave you life, and food, and a home. All who take care of you and help you were sent you by God. He sent His Son to show you His will, and to die for your sake. He gave you His word to let you know what He hath done for you, and what He wants you to do. Be sure that He sees you in the dark, as well as in the day light. He can tell all that you do, and all that you say, and all that is in your mind. Oh, ever seek this God! Pray to Him when you rise, and when you lie down. Keep His day, hear His word, and do His will, and He will love you, and will be your God for ever.'"

The Bible's influence in Lesson XX is evident, even blatant. John was admonished to work because work is good for us (Eccl. 9:10). The man for whom John worked was not painted as someone you wanted "to stick it to" (Col. 4:1). Instead he gave good advice to John as he worked (Ps. 37:30). He reminded the boy that all he had was a gift from God (Eccl. 5:18–19), including his food, his home and his ability to work (Deut. 8:18). He even made sure that John knew God sent his only Son to be the boy's Savior (John 3:16–18). He spoke positively of the influence of the Bible in John's life (Ps. 119:11, 105) and the need for John to know what God wants from him in life (1 Pet. 2:15). The ethical lesson to do what is right because God sees all we do (Jer. 16:17) and knows all we think (Dan. 2:22) was included. And the final admonition in Lesson XX was to seek God (Ps. 69:32), to hear his word (Acts 13:44), to do his will (John 13:17), and to love him (1 John 5:2).

[6] Bates, *Battleground*, 208.

remains strong today. Of the top fifty names given to girls in America in 2005, fourteen are Bible names. Of the top fifty names given to boys, twenty-five are Bible names.[7]

Towns and villages across our country also have biblical names. Whether it's Pennsylvania (Bethlehem, Nazareth, Emmaus, Bethesda, Shiloh, Bethel, Eden, Ephrata, Zionsville, and New Jerusalem), Texas (Palestine, Hebron, Eden, Joshua, Temple, Bishop, Blessing, and Corpus Christi), California (Antioch, Carmel, Goshen, Bethel Island, Joshua Tree, and Temple City),[8] or any state in between, you'll find evidence the Bible had a direct influence on the society and culture of Old America.

Speaking the Bible as a Second Language

Many common expressions we use today have their origins in the Bible. Phrases like "apple of his eye" (Deut. 32:10; Zech. 2:8); "Eat, drink, and be merry" (Eccl. 8:15 KJV), and "the blind leading the blind" (Matt. 15:14; Luke 6:39) all come from the Bible. So do dozens more.[9]

Common words like *adoption, ambitious, busybody, liberty,* and *scapegoat* were introduced into our English language through the Bible.[10] Without the influence of the Bible, English would be robbed of much of its colorful language. When we speak the English language, we truly are speaking the Bible as a second language.

The Bible's Influence on Art and Literature

Educator Allan Bloom suggests:

---

[7] For information on popular baby names, go to the Social Security web site (www.ssa.gov/OACT/babynames).

[8] This is not to mention all those Spanish "saint" names like San Andreas, San Gabriel, San Joaquin, San Juan, San Marcos, San Mateo, San Pablo, Santa Cruz or Santa Maria.

[9] "Eye for an eye"—Exodus 21:24; Leviticus 24:20; Matthew 5:38; "Good Samaritan"—Luke 10:25–37; "Handwriting on the wall"—Dan. 5:5; "My brother's keeper"—Gen. 4:9; "Out of the mouths of babes"—Ps. 8:2; "Set your house in order"—2 Kings 20:1; Isa. 38:1; "Red sky at morning"—Matthew 16:3; "Signs of the times"—Matthew 16:3; "Strait and narrow"—Matt. 7:14; "Sweat of your brow"—Gen. 3:19 KJV; "There's nothing new under the sun"—Eccl. 1:9; "Thorn in the flesh"—2 Cor. 12:7; et al.

[10] Stanley Malless and Jeffrey McQuain, *Coined by God* (New York: W. W. Norton & Co., 2003). Other words or phrases coined for the *King James Version* of the Bible include: *beautiful; bald head; castaway; cucumber; eat, drink and be merry; holier than thou; house divided; left wing; network; puberty; two-edged sword; under the sun;* and *wrinkle.*

Imagine such a young person [devoid of history, especially Bible history and the stories of the Bible] walking through the Louvre or the Uffizi, and you can immediately grasp the condition of his soul. In his innocence of the stories of Biblical and Greek or Roman antiquity, Raphael, Leonardo, Michelangelo, Rembrandt and all the others can say nothing to him. All he sees are colors and forms—modern art. In short, like almost everything else in his spiritual life, the paintings and statues are abstract.[11]

That's just as true for American art, especially folk art. In a recent article in the *Atlanta Journal-Constitution*, author Bill Osinski said, "Folk art's most dominant theme is, and always has been, religion."[12] American poetry has often been influenced by the Bible (Annie Dillard's *Pilgrim at Tinker Creek*, Emily Dickinson's *The Only News I Know*, and T. S. Eliot's *Journey of the Magi*) as has American literature (John Steinbeck's *The Grapes of Wrath*, Toni Morrison's *The Song of Solomon*, or Harriet Beecher Stowe's *Uncle Tom's Cabin*).[13]

Even the American film industry has been impacted by the Bible. Think of blockbusters such as *The Ten Commandments*, *The Passion of the Christ*, and *King of Kings*, as well as movies such as *The Matrix*, *Pulp Fiction*, and *Bruce Almighty*. Hollywood has not always treated the Bible well (*Coneheads*, *The Last Temptation of Christ*, *The DaVinci Code*), but the epic biblical tales of earlier years proved that even filmmakers were Bible-friendly, as was most of Old America.

The Bible has played a major role in the formation of our English language. Its influence on our culture is everywhere. Old American society would not be the great society it is today without the impact of the Bible.

---

[11] Allan Bloom, *The Closing of the American Mind* (New York: Simon and Schuster, 1987), 63.

[12] As examples, Myrtice West's *Crucifixion of Christ*, *Adam and Eve*, and *Portrait of the Anti-Christ*, as well as William Blayney's *Antichrist King 666* and William Gayle's *Crucifixion*.

[13] Other examples of the Bible's influence on American literature would be: Zora Neale Hurston's *Their Eyes Were Watching God*, Paul Auster's *City of Glass*, Herman Melville's *Moby Dick*, Harold Frederic's *The Damnation of Theron Ware*, William Golding's *Lord of the Flies*, and Nathaniel Hawthorne's *The Scarlet Letter*.

5

The Birth of New America

If we abide by the principles taught in the Bible, our country will go on prospering. . . . But if we and our posterity neglect its instructions and authority, no man can tell how sudden a catastrophe may over-whelm us and bury all our glory in profound obscurity.

—DANIEL WEBSTER

The place of privilege afforded the Bible in Old America continued into the twentieth century. But within two decades of the end of World War II, the influence of the Bible on America began to change, and America's attitudes and approach toward the Bible changed with it.

Old America was friendly toward the Bible. It wasn't that everybody in Old America was a Bible reader or a follower of Christ, but rather that society in general had an innate respect for the Bible. They trusted it, they believed it, and they quoted it, even if they didn't always read it.

During the 1950s immediately after the war, business, industry, and cities were all rapidly growing. This decade was also full of religious vitality, with rapid growth in church membership, especially in the booming new suburbs.[1]

A Decade of Disruption

By the early 1960s, however, new winds blew through the land of the free and the home of the brave. This decade saw major change and

---

[1] Linda Lyons, "Protestants vs. Catholics: Who's Got Religion?" *The Gallup Poll*, January 25, 2005.

upheaval for America—the assassinations of President John F. Kennedy, Martin Luther King Jr., Malcolm X, and Robert Kennedy; war protests; the beginnings of the women's liberation movement; and strong anti-establishment feelings. Those feelings may have carried over to organized religion because both Bible reading and weekly church attendance began to slide among Protestants and Catholics. By 1969 church attendance was down eleven points from 1955 among Catholics and five points among Protestants.[2]

It was also during this decade that two decisions by the United States Supreme Court played a huge role in the attitude of America toward the Bible. In *Engal v. Vitale* (1962), the United States Supreme Court ruled that prayer in public schools breached the constitutional wall of separation between church and state. And in *Abington v. Schempp* (1963), the high court found that Bible reading over the school intercom was unconstitutional.[3]

The activism of the 1960s gave way to pessimism, cynicism, and disillusionment in the 1970s. Americans questioned everything, including the Bible. There was growing pessimism about the prospects for peace in the world, the plight of the poor, and the possibility of social justice. God was seen as distant and his Word was becoming more distant as well. Catholic attendance at Mass continued to slip during this decade, from 60 percent in 1970 to 52 percent in 1979. Protestants' weekly attendance showed little change.[4]

During these decades the Bible lost its special position. There was no universally perceived need to show respect toward God's Word. The New America that developed no longer trusted the Bible,

[2] George H. Gallup Jr., "Catholics Trail Protestants in Church Attendance," *The Gallup Poll GNPS Commentary*, December 17, 2003.
[3] Subsequent Supreme Court decisions also showed an unfriendly attitude toward the Bible. *Murray v. Curlett*, (1963)—the Supreme Court found that forcing a child to participate in Bible reading and prayer was unconstitutional. *Stone v. Graham*, (1980)—the Supreme Court found posting of the Ten Commandments in schools was unconstitutional. *Alleghany County v. ACLU*, (1989)—the Supreme Court found that the nativity scene displayed inside a government building violated the Establishment Clause. *Santa Fe Independent School District v. Doe*, (2000)—the Supreme Court ruled that student-led prayers at public school football games violated the Establishment Clause of the First Amendment.
[4] George H. Gallup Jr., "Catholics Trail Protestants in Church Attendance," *The Gallup Poll GNPS Commentary*, December 17, 2003.

no longer believed it, and no longer quoted it. In fact, New America became generally hostile toward the Bible.

> The biggest decline in belief that the Bible is true and to be taken literally was in the late 1960s and early 1970s.
> —George Gallup Jr. and Jim Castelli

Flying High

The 1980s were far more upbeat. The economy began to grow, dabbling in investments became a way of life, and optimism for the future increased. Despite the continuing cold war and nuclear threat, Americans were far less apprehensive about the immediate future. However, that confidence seemed to replace a need to depend on God, and Bible reading suffered as a result. Catholic church attendance changed very little, hovering between 51 percent and 53 percent. Protestant church attendance was also static.[5]

During the 1990s, America was flying high. The economy was good, deficits were down, and expendable income was up. But this was not a good decade for the Bible or morality. Sexual scandals raged in the White House Clinton administration and also in the Catholic Church. Many people viewed the Bible as out of touch, and therefore out of sight, with everyday life. Catholic church attendance declined slightly. Meanwhile Protestant church attendance was bolstered by the megachurch movement.[6]

During the first few years of the twenty-first century, attendance at Catholic churches experienced some ups and downs, but nowhere near the declines that occurred between the 1960s and the 1980s. In March 2002, Protestants reported attending church more frequently on average than Catholics for the first time in nearly a half-century of *Gallup Poll* data collection. Protestants' levels of church attendance have remained higher than that of Catholics since then. But

---

[5] Ibid.
[6] George Gallup Jr., "Catholics Trail Protestants in Church Attendance," *The Gallup Poll GPNS Commentary*, December 16, 2003.

Bible literacy has suffered among all Christians. The decline in Bible understanding has never fallen lower in America than it is right now.[7]

George Gallup and Michael Lindsay wrote a book that documents the shallowness of American Christianity over the last five decades. Two of the underlying themes suggested by their findings are "the glaring lack of knowledge about the Bible, basic doctrines, and the traditions of one's church . . . [and] the superficiality of faith, with many people not knowing what they believe, or why."[8]

Decades of Decline

Gallup reports, "In broad terms, there was, first, a post-World War II surge of interest in religion, characterized by increased church membership and attendance, a growth in Bible reading, increased giving to churches, and extensive church building. . . . The surge lasted until the late 1950s or early 1960s, when it was replaced by a decline in religious interest and involvement in the 1960s and 1970s. Finally, the 1980s saw a "bottoming out" of certain indicators, if not a reversal of some of the decline."[9]

> While understanding the Bible is important to many people, relatively few find it important to read or listen to the Bible on a regular basis.
> —Yankelovich marketing and advocacy study, January 13, 2006

According to Gallup, "The proportion of Americans who believe the Bible is literally true fell by half in a quarter of a century. In 1963, 65 percent of Americans believed the Bible was literally true. This figure fell to 38 percent by 1978."[10] Obviously the turbulent decade of the 1960s took a toll both on reading the Bible and confidence in the Bible.

[7] Ibid.
[8] George Gallup Jr. and D. Michael Lindsay, *Surveying the Religious Landscape: Trends in U.S. Beliefs* (New York: Morehouse, 1999), 4.
[9] George Gallup Jr. and Jim Castelli, *The People's Religion* (New York: Macmillan, 1989), 5.
[10] Ibid., 61.

America had a splendid heritage in the Word of God. We built our government on it. We built our laws on it. We built our lives on it. But when we began to put the Bible on the back burner, a New America was formed. It's an America that is not friendly toward the Bible, an America that doesn't read the Bible or respect it. It's an America in which Bible illiteracy is rampant.

Sadly, it's our America. We gave it life. And now we are reaping what we have sown.

Part Three

The Bible's Declining Influence on America

If Christians blew the dust off their Bibles at the same time, we'd all be killed in the dust storm.

—WOODROW KROLL

6

What Is Bible Illiteracy?

Clearly there is a need to treat biblical illiteracy in this country with all the urgency of a medical emergency.

—GEORGE GALLUP JR.

Recently, I spent a week in Paris. Years ago, I had studied there and I've gone back many times since. And yet I found myself returning to the same places—Altitude 95 on the Eiffel Tower for dinner, Notre Dame for the choir, and the Louvre—because it's the Louvre. But perhaps my favorite spot in Paris is Sainte Chappelle.

Built by King Louis IX to house the Crown of Thorns, part of the "True Cross," and other supposed relics from the Holy Land, the chapel is almost swallowed up today by the Palais de Justice on the Ile de la Cite near Notre Dame. The climb up the spiral staircase to the second floor chapel is well worth the effort. There you see the most breathtaking stained-glass windows in the world.

The tiny chapel's walls consist almost entirely of glass—6,588 square feet of gorgeous glass. A regular stop for students on European study tours and tourists alike, everyone stands in breathless awe before the glass. But most people don't understand what they're looking at. The 1,134 scenes on the windows depict the Christian story from the Garden of Eden to the end, Genesis through Revelation. The great rose window depicts the Apocalypse. Without a knowledge of the Bible, the brilliant windows of Sainte Chappelle are just pieces of cut glass.

The same can be said of our country today concerning the Bible. In a *Los Angeles Times* article, professor of humanities at Yale

University Harold Bloom observed, "The Bible was the foundation and blueprint for our Constitution, Declaration of Independence, educational system, and our entire history until the last [twenty] to [thirty] years." If Americans do not understand the Bible, if they are Bible illiterate, then how can they understand the history and foundation of America?

Defining Bible Illiteracy and Literacy

First, let's define terms. What do we mean when we talk about Bible literacy? Is Bible literacy different from reading literacy? Can a person who is non-literate be Bible literate?

"The term 'illiteracy' immediately brings to mind the inability to read or write," says Rick Byargeon, "but in the case of Americans, it is becoming 'a lack or familiarity with language or literature.'"[1] While organizations that deal with illiteracy usually are concerned with the incapacity to read,[2] Bible illiteracy has more to do with inattention than inability. For our purposes here when I talk about Bible illiteracy in America, the definition relates to a lack of familiarity with the Bible, not to a lack of ability to read it. Bible illiteracy is not the unfortunate, unintentional inability to read and understand Scripture; it is the unfortunate, intentional neglect of Scripture.

So what is Bible literacy? Is it just reading the Bible? No, it's more. Reading is fundamental, but it isn't enough. You have to read the Bible and then interpret it and apply it to your life. Those are the initial steps in Bible literacy. They are also the first steps toward spiritual maturity.

---

[1] Rick Byargeon, "Biblical Illiteracy Confronted In Spring Hobbs Lecture," April 2, 2001, www.okbu.edu/news/hobbs01.html.

[2] The Family Literacy Council defines literacy as: "The ability to read, write and communicate in one's native language, to compute and solve problems at levels of proficiency necessary to function on the job and in society, to achieve one's goals and live to the best of one's ability" (www.4state.com/flc/literacy.htm). But according to The Literacy Action, Inc. (LAI), the current meaning of literacy in America is: "the ability to read, write and speak in English and compute and solve problems on the job and in society, to achieve one's goals and develop one's knowledge and potential" (www.literacyaction.org/about_history.asp).

> Bible literacy occurs when a person, with access to a Bible in a language he or she understands, consistently reads or hears the truth of the Word of God with personal understanding and grows toward spiritual maturity as an outcome.
>
> —Woodrow Kroll

The Bible Literacy Continuum

Early in my thinking about this, I developed a scale for Bible literacy. It's a continuum, a line along which each of us finds ourselves in relationship to how well we relate to the Bible and its Author. It's not perfect, but this scale demonstrates that there is much more to Bible literacy than simply reading. Each increment of this scale moves a person from ignorance of the Bible to full connectivity with the Author and full activity in service to him.

The Kroll Scale of Bible Literacy

–3) I have no knowledge of the Bible at all.

A Bible? What's a Bible? I have never seen a Bible before and I don't know what you're talking about.

–2) I am familiar with the Bible but have no trust in its claims or authority.

A Bible? Yes, I have one someplace, but it's just for people like my grandmother. I don't read the Bible because I don't think it's what some people claim it to be. It has no impact on my life.

–1) I am familiar with the Bible but have minimal trust in its claims or authority. I never read it or hear its truth so the Bible has little or no personal impact on my life. A Bible? Yes, I have one but there's not much in it that appeals to me. I don't know if it's what it claims to be or not. Who's to say? It has little influence on me because I don't read it.

+1) I trust in the Bible and its claims and authority but only occasionally read it or hear its truth so the Bible has only occasional personal impact on my life. A Bible? Yes, it's

God's Word. I believe it's inspired by God and should be read and obeyed, but I only occasionally get around to reading it myself. In fact, I have three copies, but I don't read any of them more than once a week.

+2) I trust in the Bible—its claims and authority—and regularly read it or hear its truth with understanding, so the Bible has regular personal impact on my life. A Bible? Yes, I have one and read it regularly. I believe it's inspired by God. I'm in a Bible-reading program at church. I also read a verse or two along with my devotional book on a fairly regular basis.

+3) I trust in the Bible—its claims and authority—and daily read it or hear its truth, so the Bible produces a passion to connect personally with the Author and induces me to share him with others. A Bible? Read it? Are you kidding? I want to know God so badly that I devour the Bible daily. I used to read a couple of verses along with my devotional but now that's not enough for me. Through reading God's Word I get to know him intimately and, as a result, I am energized to share God's story with my friends and family.

Ultimately, the goal of reading the Bible is to develop such a degree of faith in its claims and understanding of its content that you passionately connect with its Author and share him consistently with your friends and family. Anything short of this is short of the goal of Bible literacy. Bible literacy, as defined in this book, occurs when we begin to read the Word of God, gain some understanding from it, and allow it to have regular impact on our lives. That's not full-blown spiritual maturity, but neither is it the full-blown neglect of Scripture that is so prevalent in the church today. In my judgment then, Bible literacy occurs at about a +2 with the goal of moving on to a +3.

Finding Your Position

The key question you should ask yourself is: Where am I on this continuum? Am I in the *minus* column or the *plus* column? And if I am in the *plus* column, what am I receiving from my Bible that truly influences my life and connects me with God and service to him? Bible literacy does not indicate full spiritual maturity, but it is a necessary step on the road to full spiritual maturity. The path to spiritual maturity in Christ goes through the door of Bible literacy.

7

Bibles, Bibles Everywhere

We cannot assume any biblical knowledge on the part of our hearers at all: the most elementary Bible stories are completely unknown. Furthermore, the situation is getting worse.

—D. A. CARSON

The Bible remains the world's unrivaled all-time best-selling book. It seems to be just about everywhere. Yet, the American public's knowledge of the Bible remains abysmal. Have you had the opportunity to watch one of the late night "theologians"? David Letterman and Jay Leno have gone head-to-head for years in the late-night TV wars. And while they both can be tasteless or hilarious, Jay Leno does a piece on *The Tonight Show* called "Jaywalking" that is a scream.

He goes out on the street, sticks a microphone under the nose of passersby, and asks them questions. Now, granted, the producers choose the dumbest answers for airing; that's what makes good comedy. But when Bible questions are asked, the answers aren't hilarious; they're pathetic.

Leno will ask, "Name one of the Ten Commandments" and the most popular answer is, "God helps those who help themselves." With a smile Leno continues, "Name any one of the apostles." No answer. "Can you name any of the Beatles?" The immediate response: "John, Paul, George, and Ringo." Undeterred, Leno asks, "Who was swallowed by a great fish?" and the confident answer comes back, "Pinocchio."

Okay. Let's be honest. It's *The Tonight Show*. The producers do choose the looniest responses. But the obvious lack of familiarity with Bible stories and characters is not just a symptom on television; it's also a symptom of American life.

Choices and Challenges

I went on line the other day to Amazon.com to check out the choices of Bibles for sale. Do you want to guess how many there were? There were 1,035 Bibles to choose from. Unbelievable. You have more than a thousand choices of Bibles to purchase on line. There are black Bibles, burgundy Bibles, blue Bibles, even Bibles with flowered covers. You can choose a devotional Bible, a study Bible, an inspirational Bible, or an annotated Bible. Take your pick between translations—literal, dynamic equivalent, or paraphrase.

And then there's the version question. Do you want the KJV, NIV, ESV, NKJV, NLT, NASB, CEV, GNB, NIRV, RSV, NRSV, HCSB, TNIV, the Amplified Bible or *The Message*? And there are dozens more. Do you want imitation leather, bonded leather, leatherflex, cowhide, or water buffalo calfskin? And what about a Bible printed just for you? Do you need a family Bible, couples Bible, singles Bible, teen Bible, men's Bible, women's Bible, recovery Bible? The choices go on and on. It's enough to make your head spin.

> 86 percent of American households own or have a Bible.
> —*Yankelovich Monitor,* 2005

Who's Reading the Bible?

According to a 2000 Gallup poll, about six in ten Americans (59 percent) say they read the Bible at least on occasion, with the most likely readers being women, nonwhites, older people, Republicans, and political conservatives.[1]

Readership of the Bible has declined from the 1980s overall,

---

[1] Alec Gallup and Wendy W. Simmons, "Six in Ten Americans Read Bible at Least Occasionally: Percentage of frequent readers has decreased over last decade." *The Gallup Brain*, October 20, 2000.

from 73 percent to 59 percent today. And the percentage of frequent readers, that is, those who read the Bible at least once a week, has decreased slightly over the last decade, from 40 percent in 1990 to 37 percent today.[2] In terms of frequency of readership, 16 percent of Americans say they read the Bible every day, 21 percent say they read it weekly, 12 percent say they read the Bible monthly, 10 percent say less than monthly, and 41 percent say that they rarely or never read the Bible.[3] You can just feel the cold air of Bible illiteracy's brisk winter settling in on America.

Readership Demographics

According to both The Gallup Organization and The Barna Group, older people are more likely to read the Bible than are younger people. Gallup reports that 50 percent of those over the age of sixty-five read the Bible at least weekly, compared to 27 percent of people between the ages of eighteen and twenty-nine. Thirty-six percent of people in their thirties and forties read the Bible that frequently.[4] Similarly, Barna statistics show that only 30 percent of twenty-somethings have read the Bible in the past week, compared to 37 percent of thirty-somethings, 44 percent of forty-somethings, 47 percent of fifty-somethings, and 55 percent of those aged sixty and above.[5]

> **Women are 29 percent more likely to read the Bible than men.**
>
> —*The Barna Update*, March 6, 2000

Can We Trust the Numbers?

In this book you will find a lot of numbers. At times you may find yourself questioning, "Can that really be true? Can we really trust the numbers?" Often the way a question is asked determines the

---

[2] Ibid.
[3] Ibid.
[4] Ibid.
[5] "Twenty-somethings Struggle to Find Their Place in Christian Churches," *The Barna Update*, September 24, 2003.

answer. For example, when Gallup asked, "Do you happen to be a member of a church or synagogue?" Sixty-five percent said yes and 35 percent said no. But Gallup's next question was, "Did you, yourself, happen to attend church or synagogue in the last seven days, or not?" and the percent of people saying yes dropped dramatically to 41 percent while those saying no rose to 59 percent.[6]

It's evident people generally feel they should be attending church and reading the Bible, but when push comes to shove, if the numbers are skewed at all, they will be skewed upward. In general, however, while the statistics vary from poll to poll and organization to organization, the numbers usually can be trusted when more than one poll or more than one polling organization detects similar numbers. That will often be the case with the statistics presented here.

Whether we base our observations on the polling numbers, anecdotes we've heard, or what we've seen with our own eyes, there's no question there is little actual engagement with the Word. A huge disconnect exists between owning a Bible and reading it. Simply put, the number of people who claim to read the Bible isn't supported by their knowledge of the Bible. And that's a fact!

Bible Knowledge Ranks Lowest

Both The Gallup Organization and The Barna Group have done extensive research on the religious beliefs of Americans. The results of those polls do not hide the growing plague of Bible illiteracy in America. In a 2005 Barna poll, Americans were asked to rate their maturity in relation to seven dimensions of their spiritual life. The dimension in which the largest percentage of respondents considered themselves to be above average was in "maintaining healthy relationships." Among adults who claim to be Christian, almost half (48 percent) rated themselves above average in their ability both to create and to maintain a healthy relationship with others.[7] One-third

---

[6] Frank Newport, "A Look at Americans and Religion Today." *The Gallup Brain*, March 23, 2004.
[7] "Christians Say They Do Best at Relationships; Worst in Bible Knowledge," *The Barna Update*, June 14, 2005.

of adults (36 percent) also believed they are highly developed in the area of worship.[8]

But here's the stinger: the two areas of spiritual life people most readily admitted they struggle with are "sharing your faith with others" (23 percent above average, 23 percent below average, with 53 percent average) and "Bible knowledge" (21 percent above average, 25 percent below average, 53 percent average).[9]

> Of the seven dimensions in which Americans were asked to rate their faith maturity, Bible knowledge ranked dead last.
> —*The Barna Update,* June 14, 2005

Those categories where people admitted feeling they are not very mature or not at all mature in Barna's seven dimensions are: "maintaining healthy relationships" (5 percent), "consistently living your faith principles" (7 percent), "serving people" (8 percent), "worship" (14 percent), "spiritually leading your family" (14 percent), "sharing your faith with others" (23 percent), and "Bible knowledge" (25 percent).[10]

We Want to Know the Bible Better

In the Barna survey each respondent was asked to identify that dimension of their faith they would most like to improve. The most common answer was, "No particular dimension," but frequently people indicated a desire to strengthen their personal commitment to their faith (13 percent) and to increase their knowledge of the Bible (12 percent). Only these responses reached double figures.[11] So, if we want to know God's Word better, what's stopping us? We have the Bible in our own language. We have a plethora of translations and versions to choose from. What's the problem? Read on. That's what this book is about.

---

[8] Ibid.
[9] Ibid.
[10] Ibid.
[11] Ibid.

8

Why People Don't Read the Bible

Our biggest problem isn't that people think the Bible is a bad book. There are always people who hate the Bible and reject God outright, of course; but if you're like most folks, you don't hate the Bible. You think of it as the Good Book. But do you read it? Do you know what it says? Do you base your life on its teachings?

—*THE BACK TO GOD HOUR*

For years I've been tracking the reasons people give for failing to read their Bible consistently.[1] Maybe you've expressed many of them yourself. They all seem reasonable until you take a closer look. Again, in the style of David Letterman on *The Late Show*, here are the "Top Ten" reasons people tell me why they don't read the Bible. See if any of these are your reasons.

Reason 10: I Don't Know Where to Start

Why have we made an issue of where you start reading the Bible? Readers of *The Purpose-Driven Life* knew where to start. So did readers of the *Left Behind* series and *The Chronicles of Narnia*.

Here's a novel idea: start at the beginning. In the first eleven

---

[1] Yankelovich also has a list of reasons why people don't read the Bible. When they asked, "Which of the following would you say is a reason why you don't read or listen to the Bible more?" responses were: 56 percent—it's just not a habit for me; 30 percent—I forget; 27 percent—I'm too busy, I don't have time; 25—percent the language is too difficult to understand; 20 percent—I don't know where to begin; 6 percent—it's too boring; 5 percent—it doesn't seem relevant to me; 2 percent—it doesn't apply to my daily life. Yankelovich, "Scripture Engagement Operating System Product, Marketing, and Advocacy Study," Scripture Union/American Bible Society (January 13, 2006), 43.

chapters of Genesis, you'll find the answers to all the great issues of life. There you will learn whether men and women evolved from lower life forms or were "endowed by their Creator" as our founding fathers so confidently asserted in the Declaration of Independence.[2] In these first chapters you'll discover the purpose of marriage, the origins of evil, the geography of early humanity, and both the grace and judgment of God.

If you don't read your Bible because you don't know where to start, let your instincts guide you. To have the best vantage point to understand the rest of the Bible, a good place to start is at the beginning, in Genesis.

Reason 9: I Can't Find What I Want in the Bible

Have you ever been reading the Bible and said to yourself, I've read something like that before? Sometimes people are haunted by the memory of a story, a saying, or even a word and can't remember where they read it, so they give up.

Do this: Read your Bible with an open notebook, laptop, or journal nearby. When you encounter something that strikes you as particularly important or interesting, jot it down. Don't rely on your memory. An old Chinese proverb says, "The smallest amount of ink is stronger than the largest amount of memory." Write it down.

You can also use a concordance to help you find what you want. That's a book or computer program that lists every verse in the Bible in which a particular word is used. (Logos Bible Software has an incredibly complete software program of Bible study tools all in one package that will be more than you will ever use in a lifetime.)

So, don't let your inability to find one thing in the Bible keep you from reading the rest of it. The fact is, the more you read, the easier it will be to locate things.

---

[2] In the 1776 United States Declaration of Independence, Thomas Jefferson famously asserted: "We hold these truths to be self-evident, that all men are created equal, that they are endowed by their Creator with certain unalienable Rights, that among these are Life, Liberty and the pursuit of Happiness."

Reason 8: The Bible Doesn't Confirm What I Believe

A few years ago I received a letter from a radio listener in California. This young wife wrote: "I'm planning to divorce my husband because he isn't growing as fast spiritually as I am. In fact, I feel like he's holding me back. I've met this guy at our church fellowship who is already divorced. He and I are so much more compatible spiritually and I believe God may be leading us together. It feels right to me. What do you think?"

Frankly, this woman wasn't at all interested in what I thought; she simply wanted my blessing on her sin. She wasn't interested in what the Bible said either unless it agreed with what she felt was "right."

> **Many people today appear to be practicing a "do-it-yourself" faith—taking pieces from various traditions and building their own kind of "patchwork" faith.**
> —George Gallup Jr.

Some people choose not to read the Bible because they're afraid it will contradict what they've already made up their mind to do. But the Bible isn't a dialogue between God and us. It's a revelation from him to us. The Bible should be our guide to life, not a sometimes-support for our pre-existing belief system.

Reason 7: I Hear the Bible at Church, So Why Do I Need to Read It for Myself

Early Christians compensated for not having personal copies of the Scriptures by reading extensively from the Bible at each church service. That's why Paul told Timothy, "Devote yourself to the public reading of Scripture" (1 Tim. 4:13). In a period of one year the early congregations would hear the entire Bible read aloud.

Does your pastor read Scripture in his sermon? If so, does he read an entire book? Probably not. How about a chapter? Too long. Would an average of five verses be about right? If that's all the Scripture you ever read, those five verses would total 260 verses each year. If you don't read the Bible yourself because you hear it in church, you'd have to live an astonishing 120.6 years just to hear all of God's Word once.[3] Still think you don't need to read the Bible for yourself?

Reason 6: The Language of the Bible Doesn't Make Sense to Me

When I was growing up, some words in my King James Bible were more than a little difficult to understand. When I read, "Lay apart all filthiness and superfluity of naughtiness" (James 1:21 KJV), I admit I was a bit puzzled. And when someone went to the pastor admitting, "Pastor, I have been guilty of evil concupiscence" (Col. 3:5 KJV), I can remember the puzzled look on the pastor's face as he said, "Let me get back to you on that." Actually, the more I read the Bible, the less difficulty I had understanding even Elizabethan English.

Years ago it was easy to blame the language of the Bible for our lack of Bible reading. "It's King James's fault. His language is so old-fashioned. If I just had a Bible in modern English, then I'd read it." Well, now we have dozens of Bibles in easy-to-read twenty-first-century English, and we still don't read the only Book God ever wrote. There may be words and concepts in the Bible that are puzzling, but don't let that stop you from reading it. It doesn't stop you with other books.

Reason 5: The Bible Is Such a Big Book. I Could Never Read It All

The Bible is a big book. In fact, it's a library, a collection of sixty-six books. Some are quite long—Genesis, Matthew, Isaiah, Acts—but others are quite short—Philippians, Malachi, Colossians, Zephaniah. In fact, five books in this library have only one chapter.[4] One book has just two chapters.[5]

Perhaps you view the Bible the way you view Tolstoy's *War*

---

[3] In the *King James Version* of the Bible there are 31,373 verses.
[4] Obadiah, Philemon, 2 John, 3 John, and Jude.
[5] Haggai.

and Peace. You know it's a classic, you know you should try to read it and you don't have anything against it, but it's so long and it looks so imposing you just never get around to it. Leo Tolstoy's *War and Peace* contains fifteen books, 365 chapters, and 1,300 pages.

But is the length of the books in the Bible really the reason why people don't read them? Did you read any of the Harry Potter books? The first, *Harry Potter and the Sorcerer's Stone*, was the shortest at 309 pages. By book four, *Harry Potter and the Goblet of Fire*, J. K. Rowling was up to 734 pages. Book five, *Harry Potter and the Order of the Phoenix,* was 870 pages. No excuses there.

I subscribe to *Christianity Today* (*CT*) and several other magazines. If you exclude the pages of ads and other nonsubstantive pages and read only the articles, letters to the editors, and special features, you will read about 355,000 words in the twelve monthly issues of *CT*. That's about half as many words as are found in the Bible.[6]

Many of us read several magazines, lots of newspapers, and a few good books every year, but when it comes time to reading the Bible, we say it's too long. I don't think God is buying that.

Reason 4: The Bible Isn't Relevant to My Life

Bill Armstrong was a young businessman in my church. His partner and he sold and installed security systems in homes. Bill was a Christian but Jack, his partner, was not. A conflict arose between them because Jack wanted to up-sell customers to a more expensive product that wasn't as good as the cheaper model. Bill was hesitant and wanted to check out his Bible for advice, but he didn't know where to look.[7]

One day Bill came to me. I steered him to some passages where

---

[6] There are approximately 775,693 words in the *King James Version* of the Bible.
[7] God told the Israelites always to be fair in business. "You shall not have in your bag differing weights, a heavy and a light" (Deut. 25:13 NKJV), implying that some merchants would cheat their customers with a weight that was lighter than the standard. Paul told the Corinthian believers to do all things honestly and honorably, "not only in the sight of the Lord, but also in the sight of men" (2 Cor. 8:21 NKJV).

God told the Israelites always to be fair in business (e.g., Deut. 25:13; 2 Cor. 8:21). When he left, Bill knew what he had to do. He bought Jack's interest in their business (2 Cor. 6:14) and quit selling the over-priced but inferior alarm systems. People appreciated Bill's honesty and today his business is booming.

The Bible's relevance to us isn't determined by what it says; it's determined by what we know of what it says and whether we live what we know. If you can't put your finger on any passages of Scripture that speak to your needs, that doesn't mean there aren't any. If you become more familiar with the Bible, it will bring more relevance to you.

Reason 3: The Bible Is Boring and Wasn't Written to Me Anyway

If some portions of the Bible seem boring to you, you're not alone. Even a spiritual giant like John Bunyan, author of the classic Christian allegory *Pilgrim's Progress*, once said, "I have sometimes seen more in a line of the Bible than I could well tell how to stand under, and yet at another time the whole Bible hath been to me as dry as a stick." Bunyan's candor is exactly the point. There are por-tions of the Bible that are not as exciting as others—Leviticus, Ezekiel, Obadiah—but the whole Bible isn't like that. Let's be fair. You may have to slosh through some places in Scripture, but the vast majority of the Bible has ready application for your life.

In the Bible you will find love stories (Isaac and Rebekah, Jacob and Rachel, Joseph and Mary), war stories (Joshua and the Amalekites, Hezekiah and the Assyrians, David and the Philistines), stories of international intrigue (Daniel, Moses, the Magi), and sto-ries of family conflict (Jacob and his sons, the prodigal and his father, Cain and Abel). You'll also read of death threats (Mordecai), attempts on one's life (Paul), and even a story about a boy king hid-den from his grandmother so she wouldn't kill him (Joram and Athaliah). So what's your interest? The Bible has it all—danger, intrigue, passion, jealousy, betrayal, love, honor. It's all in there. The Bible is anything but boring.

Reason 2: Reading the Bible Isn't a Priority in My Life

In our "Top Ten" list, the reasons for not reading the Bible are becoming both more revealing and more honest. How much you read your Bible depends on how valuable you think that time in the Word will be.

> 27 percent of Frequent Bible Readers, 30 percent of Infrequent Bible Readers, and 60 percent of Non-Readers are satisfied with the amount of time they spend reading the Bible.
>
> —Yankelovich marketing and advocacy study, January 13, 2006

Suppose you were having chest pains and your family finally convinced you to see your physician. The doctor told you to quit smoking, to get more exercise, and to eat a healthier diet, or you would soon die. Your responses could be to discount everything this trained professional told you and continue your chosen lifestyle. You could modify the doctor's instructions by doing just some of what was said. Or you could take the doctor's warning seriously and make certain lifestyle changes immediately in order to extend both the quality and quantity of your life. Which option you chose would depend on how much this was a priority to you.

The same is true in reading your Bible. The words that come from God provide spiritual life for you. Solomon said, "Trust in the LORD with all your heart, and do not lean on your own understanding. In all your ways acknowledge him, and he will make straight your paths. Be not wise in your own eyes; fear the LORD, and turn away from evil. It will be healing to your flesh and refreshment to your bones" (Prov. 3:5–8).

We get done whatever is a priority for us to get done. For those who want to live physically, they do what their doctor tells them. For those who want to live spiritually, they do what the Bible tells them. But unless the Word becomes a priority in our lives, we'll never seek its wisdom.

As Tim Morrill, founder of the Fellowship in His Love ministry, says, "Today, unless you were brought up under a rock, or in a Stone Age tribe in a jungle somewhere, you know in your heart that there is a book called the Holy Bible you should be reading. Biblical illiteracy is 99.9 [percent] a matter of choice."[8]

Reason 1: I Don't Have Time to Read the Bible

The most common excuse for not reading the Bible is our busy lives. We don't seem to have time to do the things we need to do. There's work and school, running to the store, soccer practice, dinner—life is just a bit harried. Who has time to sit and read?

You do. Here's why: time is a set quantity. It's not elastic. We all have sixty seconds in every minute, sixty minutes in every hour, twenty-four hours in every day. Time may fly, but it doesn't change. You have 1,440 golden minutes in every day and so do I.

> **41 percent of Bible readers experience the frustration of never seeming to have enough time to read.**
> —The Barna Group, June 2000

The issue is never about time; it's always about what we choose to get done in the time we have. Is reading God's Word, meditating and benefiting from it, something you wish to take the time to do or not? If not, the convenient but pathetic excuse is to say, "I don't have time."

A couple of years ago, I took a stopwatch with me everywhere I flew. I would read my Bible while in flight and time how long it took to read each book of the Bible. Once when I was returning from Frankfurt on a flight to Chicago, a flight attendant saw the stopwatch and asked, "Are you timing our service?" I chuckled and said, "No, I'm timing how long it takes me to read my Bible." Puzzled, she asked why someone would want to do that. I said, "Because everybody tells me they would read their Bible but they don't have time. I want to know how much time they don't have."

---

[8] *The High Cost of Illiteracy*, www.fellowshipinhislove.com/illiteracy.html.

Did you know that you can read half the books of the Bible in less than thirty minutes each? You can read twenty-six of them in less than fifteen minutes. The whole Bible, cover to cover, can be read by an average reader in less than seventy-two hours.

Maybe it's time we rethink our reasons for not reading the Bible and just call them what they are—excuses. Take another look at these "Top Ten." How many of them have you used with God as an excuse for not reading his Word? If you can see through the excuses so quickly, imagine how easily he can see through them. The Bible is read by people who choose to read it. Bible reading is neglected by people who choose to neglect it. It's just that simple.

No excuses. Just honesty.

Part Four

The Spreading Famine of Bible Illiteracy

Bible illiteracy is not a problem in the church. Bible illiteracy is the problem in the church.

—WOODROW KROLL

9

The Spreading Famine and the Christian

Americans revere the Bible—but, by and large, they don't read it. And because they don't read it, they have become a nation of biblical illiterates.

—GEORGE GALLUP JR.

Long before September 11 we should have been concerned about homeland security. Not the anti-terrorist kind of concern; the concern for the security of Bible knowledge in our homeland.

Much of the research of The Barna Group over the last few years has been aimed at taking the pulse of the faith of Americans, especially Americans who claim to be "born again" or evangelicals. Significant portions of that research demonstrate that in almost every category there is little difference between the "born-again" segment of American society and everyone else. Their values are essentially the same.

What about knowledge of the Bible? Let's examine whether or not Christians do better than non-Christians in reading the Bible, absorbing its message, and applying its truths to their lives.

Barna Research

The following analysis of "born-again" evangelical faith is based on the research of The Barna Group. Barna never asks respondents to their polls to define or describe their religious tradition; they are only asked to describe their faith beliefs. Barna then assigns faith values to respondents based on their answers to the questions asked. Thus, "born-again Christians" are defined as people who said they've made "a personal commitment to Jesus Christ that is still important in their life today," and who also indicated they believe that when they die they'll go to heaven because they had "confessed their sins and had accepted Jesus Christ as their Savior."[1]

"Evangelicals" are a subset of "born-again Christians" in Barna surveys. In addition to meeting the born-again criteria, evangelicals also meet seven other conditions, including saying their faith is very important in their life today, that eternal salvation is only possible through grace, and that the Bible is totally accurate in all it teaches.[2] Being classified as "evangelical" is not dependent upon any church or denominational affiliation or involvement.[3]

"Born-Again" Evangelicals Are Better Than the Average

There is good news. It will come as no surprise that evangelicals do much better than the Christian or Protestant population in general both in Bible reading and biblical understanding.

> Evangelicals are three times more likely than the national average to attend Sunday school (58%), three-and-a-half times more likely to share their faith in Christ (75%), three times as likely to belong to a small group (58%), and twice as likely to attend church in a typical week (79%).
> —*The Barna Update*, March 18, 2003

While evangelicals maintain quite a strong faith system, there is significant erosion of truth among the "born-again" segment of the

---

[1] "Barna Survey Reveals Significant Growth in Born Again Population," *The Barna Update*, March 27, 2006.

[2] The seven criteria The Barna Group imposes on "born-again" Americans to qualify as "evangelicals" are: (1) saying their faith is very important in their life today; (2) contending that they have a personal responsibility to share their religious beliefs about Christ with non-Christians; (3) stating that Satan exists; (4) maintaining that eternal salvation is possible only through grace, not works; (5) asserting that Jesus Christ lived a sinless life on earth; (6) saying that the Bible is totally accurate in all it teaches; and (7) describing God as the all-knowing, all-powerful, perfect deity who created the universe and still rules it today.

[3] *The Barna Update*, March 27, 2006.

church at large. Let's consider some areas in which the erosion of biblical influence is evident.

Erosion of Truth Sources

Almost everyone in the United States believes that truth exists. However, a large majority of both adults and teenagers, Christian and non-Christian, contend that there is no absolute moral truth. More than two out of three adults and more than four out of five teenagers argue that truth is always relative to the individual and circumstances.[4]

According to a 2002 Barna survey, 44 percent of adults contend that "the Bible, the Koran and the Book of Mormon are all different expressions of the same spiritual truths."[5] This Barna survey also discovered that most Americans believe "truth can be discovered only through logic, human reasoning and personal experience." This is at odds with the Bible.

More than four out of five Americans claim to be Christian. Half of them can be classified as "born-again Christians."[6] Yet, six out of ten Americans (59 percent) reject the existence of Satan, indicating that the devil is merely a symbol of evil. This belief is embraced by both Protestants (55 percent) and Catholics (75 percent).[7] In addition, a large minority of Americans (42 percent) believe that when Jesus Christ was on earth he committed sins.[8]

> **50 percent of born-again Christians believe that a person can earn salvation based upon good works.**
> —*The Barna Update*, October 8, 2002

---

[4] "Barna Identifies Seven Paradoxes Regarding America's Faith," *The Barna Update*, December 17, 2002.

[5] "Americans Draw Theological Beliefs from Diverse Points of View," *The Barna Update*, October 8, 2002.

[6] "One-Quarter of Self-Described Born-Again Adults Rely on Means Other Than Grace to Get to Heaven," *The Barna Update*, November 29, 2005.

[7] *The Barna Update*, October 8, 2002.

[8] Ibid.

One of the greatest contradictions in what "born again" Americans believe is in the area of eternal existence. Of those who are "born again," 10 percent believe that people are reincarnated after death and 29 percent claim it is possible to communicate with the dead.[9] "Many committed born-again Christians believe that people have multiple options for gaining entry to heaven," says Barna. "They are saying, in essence, 'Personally, I am trusting Jesus Christ as my means of gaining God's permanent favor and a place in heaven—but someone else could get to heaven based upon living an exemplary life.'"[10]

Erosion of Biblical Worldview

A worldview is the way you look at everything in the world, the filter through which you interpret world events, and the glasses through which you view all experience.[11] We should expect Christians to have a worldview that is filtered through the pages of God's Word. While that expectation is logical, it is not valid.

Everyone has a worldview, but in a survey of 2,033 adults, The Barna Group discovered that relatively few American adults (only 4 percent) have a biblical worldview as the basis of their belief and decision-making process, and only 9 percent of born-again Christians have a biblical worldview.[12] The most prevalent alternative worldview to the biblical one was postmodernism. "Over the past 20 years we have seen the nation's theological views slowly become less aligned with the Bible," says Barna. "Americans still revere the Bible and like to think of themselves as Bible-believing people, but the evidence suggests otherwise."[13]

---

[9] "Americans Describe Their Views about Life After Death," *The Barna Update*, October 21, 2003.

[10] Ibid.

[11] For the purposes of research by The Barna Group, a biblical worldview is defined as believing that absolute moral truths exist, that such truth is defined by the Bible, and firm belief in six specific religious views: i.e., that Jesus Christ lived a sinless life, God is the all-powerful and all-knowing Creator of the universe and he stills rules it today, salvation is a gift from God and cannot be earned, Satan is real, Christians have a responsibility to share their faith in Christ with other people, and the Bible is accurate in all of its teachings.

[12] "A Biblical Worldview Has a Radical Effect on a Person's Life," *The Barna Update*, December 1, 2003.

[13] "Americans Draw Theological Beliefs from Diverse Points of View," *The Barna Update*, October 8, 2002.

It is obvious that while the "born-again" evangelical Christians are more biblically literate than their non-believing counterparts, it is equally obvious that evangelicals have not escaped the damage done by Bible illiteracy in America. We can't hide any longer. We have to face facts. Bible illiteracy is eating the church alive and getting hungrier all the time. We can't wait any longer to do something about it.

10

The Spreading Famine and the Church

While America's evangelical Christians are rightly concerned about the secular worldview's rejection of biblical Christianity, we ought to give some urgent attention to a problem much closer to home— biblical illiteracy in the church. This scandalous problem is our own, and it's up to us to fix it.

—R. ALBERT MOHLER JR.

Recently I was in southern California talking with pastors, church leaders, and seminary professors about Bible illiteracy in America. A friend, Carmen Mayell, traveled with me and set up all our appointments in advance by telephone or e-mail. He was shocked when some pastors, hearing we wanted thirty minutes to talk about Bible illiteracy, responded, "Well, that's not a problem in my church." But an unwillingness even to consider that the problem may exist is a problem in itself.

I don't say that as an outsider looking in but as an insider looking around me. I began my ministry as a pastor in Massachusetts. My father was the pastor for thirty-three years at a church in Pennsylvania. My older brother has been the senior pastor at his church in Virginia for more than twenty years. My son is a senior pastor at his church in Florida. I am surrounded by pastors and churches. I wouldn't have it any other way.

Loyal to the Local Church

I believe the church is God's primary agency on earth to carry out his foremost work on earth. I believe at that enormously important event at Pentecost when the Holy Spirit gave those first-century believers power from on high (Acts 2:1–4), God started something that will not end until the Lord himself returns (Acts 1:11).

Having said that, however, I do think it's well past time we stopped spending so much on church buildings and start spending more on building the church. The church needs revival. But every great revival in the Bible was accompanied by, if not initiated by, the rediscovery of God's Word (see, e.g., 2 Kings 22:1–23:25; Neh. 8:1–18; Acts 2:14–42). More than anything, the church of the twenty-first century needs to fall in love again with the Word of God.

The Conundrum of the Twenty-first-Century Church

The great mystery of the church today is whether it is dying or thriving. Are churches doing well or poorly? A growing body of research indicates that church attendance is not increasing in America, even though large churches are. The Barna Group reports that church attendance figures are in "significant decline from the early Nineties, when close to half of all adults were found in churches on Sunday."[1] The Gallup Organization reports healthier attendance but also includes those attending a synagogue and mosque along with those attending church.[2] Look around you the next time you're in church. What do you see on people's faces? What gender is most of the congregation? What is the most common age group?

> Since 1991, the U.S. adult population has grown by 15 percent but the number of adults who do not attend church has nearly doubled, rising from 39 million to 75 million—a 92 percent increase.
> —*The Barna Update*, May 4, 2004

[1] "The State of the Church, 2000," *The Barna Update*, March 21, 2000.
[2] Frank Newport, "Church Attendance Lowest in New England, Highest in South," *The Gallup Poll*, April 27, 2006.

Research shows that Baby Busters, who range from age eighteen to thirty-four, are notably less likely than older adults to attend services (28 percent compared to 51 percent of adults fifty-five or older).[3] No surprise there. But there are three surprises—three trends in church attendance—that are worthy of notice.

Teen Church Attendance

First the good news: teenagers have healthier church attendance than do their parents. More than seven out of ten teens are engaged in some church-related activity in a typical week.[4] The bad news is that when The Barna Group asked teens to estimate how likely they were to continue their church activity once they left home and were on their own, the numbers drop like a rock.[5] This, of course, is not good news for the church and one of the reasons whey we must get serious about instilling a love for God and his Word in our young people. If they are the future of the church, what is the church's future?

Twenty-Something Church Attendance

A second surprise is with the next older demographic group—the twenty-somethings. From age twenty to twenty-nine, people make many of the decisions that shape their lives forever. For many twenty-somethings, allegiance to Christian churches is a casualty of their efforts to "create their own version of fulfillment."[6]

The research shows that Americans aged twenty to twenty-nine are significantly less likely than any other age group to attend church, to donate to churches, or to read their Bible. Only three out of ten twenty-somethings (31 percent) attend church in a typical week, compared to four out of ten of those in their thirties (42 percent) and

---

[3] *The Barna Update*, March 21, 2000.
[4] "Teenagers Embrace Religion but Are Not Excited about Christianity," *The Barna Update*, January 10, 2000.
[5] Ibid.
[6] "Twentysomethings Struggle to Find Their Place in Christian Churches," *The Barna Update*, September 24, 2003.

nearly half of all adults age forty and older (49 percent). That's not good news for the church.[7]

> **Only 30 percent of twenty-somethings have read the Bible in the last week.**
> —*The Barna Update*, September 24, 2003

A decline in Bible reading parallels the twenty-somethings' decline in church attendance. The numbers of consistent Bible readers are about 33 percent less among twenty-somethings than among older adults.[8]

Senior Adult Church Attendance

The third big surprise: older Americans are dropping out of church and organized faith activities in record numbers. Barna believes this is the result of two converging trends: the limited mobility and declining health of the spiritually devout *Seniors* generation and the erosion of commitment among the less faith-driven *Builders* generation.[9] However, I believe there is a third reason why seniors are the fastest group dropping out of church.

The evangelical church has effectively abandoned its seniors by focusing on a younger audience. Seniors feel that church has been stolen from them. All that was familiar to them has been taken away. We force them to stand for long periods of time as we repeatedly sing praise choruses with which they are unfamiliar. When the church does provide a program for its seniors, the program is often condescending, designed to keep them busy but denying them vital ministry. They feel like they've been shoved aside and so they simply drop out of church.

---

[7] Ibid.
[8] Ibid.
[9] "America's Faith *Is* Changing—But Beneath the Surface," *The Barna Update*, March 18, 2003.

What Does It All Mean?

The dilemma of the twenty-first century church is that on Sunday morning the evangelical church in America appears to be stronger than ever. At the same time, however, in many evangelical churches today our two most important demographic groups are "iffy" about their future involvement in the church. Teenagers are here today, but may be planning to be gone tomorrow if the church doesn't find something of spiritual substance to give them. Our seniors are here today but feel less and less inclined to stay for tomorrow.

> 40 percent of adults attend a church service on a typical Sunday. In the early [19]90s, that number was close to half of all adults.
> —*The Barna Update*, March 5, 2001

The battle we face is not for the superstructure or even the infrastructure of the church; the battle is for the church's heart and soul. Much of the church's efforts and finances are spent on the postmodern issue of style; much of the church's future depends on the spiritual issue of substance. All this means the church needs to quickly recover Bible literacy. I can envision a future church filled with worshipers but devoid of disciples if we don't call the American church back to the Bible.

11

The Spreading Famine and Christian Ministry

The person who enters the room by leaning on an infirm door may get a reputation for violence, but the condition of the door did have something to do with his precipitous entry.

—JOHN KENNETH GALBRAITH

In the pages that follow, I make some observations as a Christian who's lived during all five decades of the decline in Bible literacy and been involved in ministry during four of them. These are observations, nothing more. But since I am a Christian who is a member of the local church, and since I work every day in Christian media and have dozens of books in print, my comments come from the inside. These are not observations of an outsider but an insider who is worried about the dumbing down of the Christian community *by* the Christian community.

Bible illiteracy never has been on the agenda of the church; it's the people's choice. No one, to my knowledge, in any Christian endeavor has intentionally collaborated to advance Bible illiteracy; but unintentionally we all have. Without wanting to, we all have played some role in dumbing down the church. The process has been subtle, largely unnoticed. I repeat: it has been unintentional. But, nevertheless, it has been relentless and deadly.

The View From Inside

Let's explore how the Christian world has contributed to our lack of Bible literacy. While it would be unfair to blame solely any one segment of Christian ministry for Bible illiteracy in America, we all have to take our share of responsibility. To draw upon John Kenneth Galbraith's statement, the condition of contemporary ministry does have something to do with the condition of contemporary Bible illiteracy.

> Nearly half of all adults—46 percent—listen to a Christian radio broadcast in a typical month.
> —*The Barna Update*, March 14, 2005

I love the media—print, TV, radio, DVDs, CDs, the Internet—all media. I intend to utilize any medium God makes available to preach the gospel. But I also know that postmodernism has had an impact on the Christian media. I want to focus on one medium—radio— because subtly and imperceptibly, radio has morphed from an instructional to an entertainment medium. The result is still good radio, but the unintended by-product has been Bible illiteracy.

The Barna Group estimates that four out of ten adults (39 percent) listen to some Christian radio programming during the course of a typical week. More amazing is that one-third of the listening base (36 percent) are not born-again Christians.[1] Radio is a perfect medium to reach people with the gospel of Jesus Christ and teach them the Word of God.

The Natural Fit of Music and Radio

Early Christian radio was primarily Bible teaching.[2] But with the growth of radio stations also came the growth of the Christian music

---

[1] *The Barna Update*, January 25, 1999.

[2] KDKA in Pittsburgh, Pennsylvania, was both the first commercial radio station and the first to broadcast a church service, when Rev. Lewis B. Whittemore, associate pastor of the Calvary Episcopal Church in Pittsburgh, broadcast directly from the church the first Sunday of the new year, 1921. A year later Rev. Paul Rader began broadcasting over WBBM in Chicago for fourteen hours each Sunday. And the year after that, R. R. Brown broadcast his Sunday service from the Omaha Gospel Tabernacle over station WOW in Omaha, Nebraska. In the 1930s Walter A. Maier began *The Lutheran Hour* and Charles E. Fuller the *Old Fashioned Revival Hour*, followed by the *Radio Bible Class* with M. R. DeHaan, the *Heaven and Home Hour* with Clarence Erickson, *Haven of Rest* with Paul Myers, and *Back to the Bible* with Theodore Epp. With the work of these intrepid pioneers, Bible teaching on radio was off to the races.

industry. I enjoy listening to Christian music via radio. Who doesn't? It's not only good entertainment, it's good ministry as well. But as music grew in popularity, and people wanted more music on the radio, station managers were in a quandary. What to do? They only had twenty-four hours to work with. Arbitron ratings[3] began to reveal that stations playing more music were beating out stations that played less. Many station managers were forced to make a choice between entertainment and instruction.

For the most part, it was not the station owner or station manager who moved radio formats to less Bible and more music. It was you and me. Some stations and networks like Moody Broadcasting Network chose a middle-of-the-road approach, programming half music and half teaching. Some went to teaching and music "blocks." Others programmed exclusively Bible teaching along with Christian news and information, like Bott Radio Network. And still others went to an all-music format.

K-LOVE, AIR1 and WAY-FM are all good examples of the work of successful radio entrepreneurs. These outlets thrive on twenty-four hours of music every day. Salem Radio Network opted to develop two unique formats. When they purchase stations in a new market, they usually buy one FM station for their all-music Fish Network and one AM station for their teaching/talk format.

The Success of the Music Format

Overall, Christian radio continues to grow. Here are some numbers from the 2006 Arbitron ratings that will give you a quick snapshot of Christian radio in America today:

- 1,093 religious radio stations in America air a music format

---

[3] Arbitron Inc. is an international media and marketing research firm serving radio broadcasters, radio networks, cable companies, advertisers, advertising agencies, outdoor advertising companies, and the online radio industry in the United States, Mexico, and Europe. Through their Scarborough Research joint venture with VNU, Arbitron also helps media companies, advertisers, and marketers understand media audiences and reach consumers more effectively. Their services and software help clients make sense of the marketplace and turn information into revenue and grow their business. For a radio program producer (like *Back to the Bible*), Arbitron identifies how many people are listening to your program on any given station at any given hour of the day.

- 815 stations air a teaching/talk format
- 55 percent of religious radio stations have a mix of the two formats
- Religious radio has seen a growth of 14 percent in the number of stations just since the dawn of the new millennium.[4]

These are excellent numbers. So why does Bible literacy continue to decline? Much of Christian radio has successfully transitioned from Bible teaching to music, and many stations have been wildly successful with that format. But this transition has not helped Bible literacy in America. Music is inspirational but temporal; God's Word is instructional and eternal.

The dramatic changes that have taken place over the last decade have had unintended consequences. The contemporary Christian music you listen to on radio is inspirational, uplifting, and generally has a message. But as beneficial as Christian music can be, when it comes to evangelism, spiritual maturity, growth in faith, and preparing to give an answer for the hope within you, music is no match for the Bible. Christian music may feature God's Word, but the Bible *is* God's Word.

There is a direct correlation between how much time we spend in God's Word—reading it and learning from it—and how literate we are in the Bible. Instead of Christian media plugging the hole in the Bible-literacy dyke, we have actually enlarged it without intending to.[5]

Since we have focused on Christian radio, let's remember there are other media that have gone through similar transitions. None of these set out to decrease the amount of Bible. They simply responded to listeners' or readers' preferences. But the result was

---

[4] Religious radio stations grew from 1,769 in 2000 to 2,014 in 2005.

[5] Recently Chuck Colson in "The Back Page" column in *Christianity Today* vented his frustration at music's takeover of Christian radio. Colson sighs, "I'm convinced that much of the music being written for the church today reflects an unfortunate trend—slipping across the line from worship to entertainment. This trend is evident not just in theater-like churches. . . . It's also true of Christian radio, historically an important source of serious preaching and teaching. Several stations recently—many acting on the advice of a leading consulting firm—have dropped serious programming in favor of all-music formats. What is the job of Christian radio, after all? To give people what they want, or—as with any ministry—to give them what they need? Music is important in the life of the church and can inspire us to focus on Christ. But it cannot take the place of solid teaching." Charles Colson, "Soothing Ourselves to Death" in *Christianity Today*, April 2006, www.ctlibrary.com/2006/April/15.116.html.

the same. We have often moved from teaching to entertainment, from substance to style.

Publishing for the Heart

So much of publishing today is publishing for the heart—the emotional part of us—and that's not bad. But if it's publishing for the heart only, and not also publishing for the mind, Bible illiteracy will find a crack to sneak through. Publishers today have to resort to more sensational titles just to catch the Christian readers' attention.[6] It's classic postmodernism where style often wins out over substance. As with all Christian media, in Christian publishing we are amusing ourselves to death. We allow what is admittedly good to rob us of what is best.

Some in Christian publishing seem to have lost their way. Many have not, for which we can thank God. But growing numbers of Christian publishers are owned by larger parent corporations that often see the Christian population as just another niche market. Christian publishers want to minister to God's people, but they need to make a profit or they won't stay in business. That's legitimate. They need to keep their eye on market trends, readers' tastes, and what's hot and what's not. Fiction is hot; Bible is not. Trendy stuff is hot; Bible stuff is not.

If a Christian publisher is to stay in business, he must match his company's book list with the cravings of the Christian public. Christian publishers are in the same catch-22 that Christian radio stations are in. If they don't give a biblically illiterate public what it wants, the publishers will go out of business.

Selling to the Heart

Christian bookstores are big business. They provide a valuable service. We all enjoy them, including me. And, without intending to,

---

[6] It's interesting that books titled: *The History of Israel*; *The Cross in the New Testament*; or *Mere Christianity* have given way to titles such as: *Bad Girls of the Bible*; *Look Great, Feel Great*; *Sisterchicks in Gondolas*.

Christian bookstores have also contributed to creeping Bible illiteracy. Like Christian radio, by offering what is entertaining, cute, and enjoyable, the Christian public has been deprived of what they need to grow to spiritual maturity. These products haven't gotten us off the road; it's more that they've steered us into a cul-de-sac and delayed our arrival.

Christian publishers, bookstores, and authors are bound together in a professional organization known as the Christian Booksellers Association (CBA). CBA president Bill Anderson wrote an article in the *Bookstore Journal*, CBA's monthly trade magazine. The article was entitled "Make a Difference with Truth" and included the following pleas. "Suppliers, I urge you to produce books, music, and products that address the important issues of truth and moral absolutes. . . . Retailers . . . I urge you to create a new category section and display products that teach, explain, and elevate the importance of truth."[7]

As a listening and reading public, we have shown little interest in stamping out personal Bible illiteracy, at least with the choices we've made. Please understand. I have dozens of books in print myself, and I certainly don't want to discourage you from reading Christian books of all kinds. My point is not that we shouldn't read Christian books or listen to Christian radio. My point is that listening to Christian music and reading Christian books should not replace reading God's Book.

Neither radio nor publishing executives intended to dumb down the Christian. But when the Bible slipped from the central focus of ministry, the result was exactly that. As the cartoon character Pogo observed, "We have met the enemy and he is us."

---

[7] Bill Anderson, "Make a Difference with Truth," *Bookstore Journal*, November 1995, 7.

Part Five

The Impact of Bible Illiteracy on America

The reason America has lost its moral moorings is because it has lost its biblical bearings.

—WOODROW KROLL

12

Bible Illiteracy Leaves Life's Key Questions Unanswered

If you are a Christian, you should have the Bible "running out of your ears." Most people only read a certain number of verses for some devotional thoughts, not to know what the book is actually saying.

—J. I. PACKER

Many people say there are just too many unanswered questions in life. But the real questions of life, the serious questions, are not left unanswered. If we fail to get answers to our most painful questions, it is not due to the silence of God but to our failure to read his Word.

One of the consequences of Bible illiteracy is that those searching for answers to the great questions of life are left clueless. Without God's eternal Word, they have no place to go for certain truth. Questioners are left to wonder about the deep things of life or, worse, to rely on the explanations of people who change their minds as often as some baseball players change teams.

The Bible addresses to one degree or another all of the universal questions of life. It is not the purpose of this book to provide detailed answers to life's most difficult questions. Others have done that.[1] However, let's take a quick look at seven questions that go

---

[1] Two web sites you may find useful in answering many of your questions about the Bible or the Christian faith are www.probe.org and www.freedompca.org/questions.htm.

unanswered because people simply are not familiar enough with God's Word to know what God has said.

Question 1: How Can I Know the Truth?

This question is really at the foundation of all other questions. If we don't have a reliable source of information, how will we know that any answer to any question is the right one? The Bible hits this question head on. When Jesus Christ stood before Pontius Pilate, he said, "I have come into the world—to bear witness to the truth" (John 18:37). Pilate's response: "What is truth?" (v. 38). But Jesus had just told him. There is only one source of truth in the universe. All truth proceeds from the Most High God. And his Son, Jesus Christ, came to identify it and share that truth.

> 83 percent of teenagers said moral truth depends on the circumstances; only 6 percent said moral truth is absolute.
> —*The Barna Update,* February 12, 2002

Steven Covey, author of *The 7 Habits of Highly Effective People*, was on the Oprah Winfrey show. He asked the studio audience to close their eyes and point north. When they opened their eyes again, they were all pointing in wildly different directions. Then Covey pulled out a compass and said, "This is how we know which way is north. You can't know from within yourself."

You can't know truth from within yourself; you need something you can trust that points to it. The way to determine right from wrong is to read God's compass, the Bible. That's where you'll find truth. If you fail to read God's Word, you're left without an answer to Pilate's question, "What is truth?"

Question 2: Does God Really Exist?

The first verse of the Bible, instead of advancing an argument or definition of God, simply says, "In the beginning, God created the heavens and the earth" (Gen. 1:1). Period. End of sentence. No argument. Rather than prove God, the Bible reveals him, tells us what he is like, what his plans and promises are for us. From the Bible we learn that:

- God is personal—he is not a thing, power, force, or influence, but a living personal being (Jer. 10:10).
- God is eternal—he has no beginning or end. "From everlasting to everlasting you are God" (Ps. 90:2).
- God is independent—ultimately every other living being is dependent on God, but he is totally independent of his creation (Acts 17:25).
- God is holy—he is separate from all others, majestic in holiness, awesome in glory (Ex. 15:11). There is none holy like the Lord (1 Sam. 2:2).
- God is just—the Lord is a God of justice. Righteousness and justice are the very foundation of his throne (Isa. 30:18; Ps. 97:2).
- God is perfect—in every sense of the word, his character, knowledge, judgments, Word, and more are all perfect (Rom. 11:33; Ps. 19:7).
- God is sovereign—he is the sole and supreme ruler of the universe and nothing whatsoever is outside of his control (Ps. 135:6; Eph. 1:11).

Get to know the Bible and you get to know God. You won't have to argue about him.

Question 3: Why Is There Evil?

Let's face it: life is full of trouble and heartache. One of the reasons many of us go through life asking, Why is life so unfair? is that we don't understand what life is all about. So why is it like that?

Read the first two chapters of Genesis. The Garden of Eden was a perfect place. Adam and Eve had everything they needed. So what happened to God's "very good" creation? Sin happened. Read Genesis 3:6 and look at the powerful words in the text immediately after it. There Adam and Eve disobeyed God and the results of mankind's sin were fear (3:10), shame (v. 10), deception (v. 13), enmity (v. 15), pain (v. 16), curse (v. 17), death (v. 19), and more—all the "unfair" things we experience today. Sin caused that evil, not God. God didn't create sin and the consequences of it. Disobedience to God caused sin and the suffering and death we see all around us.

Now you might be thinking, *but if God is so loving, why doesn't he put a stop to this?* Read the Bible and you'll find out. It's all in there. God will put a stop to sin and its consequences. It's a part of his redemptive plan (John 3:16; 14:1–3; Rev. 11:15; 21:4; 22:3). Not knowing the Bible causes us to question God needlessly and often foolishly. It's as if God laid out all the answers for us in an instruction manual, and we didn't take the time to read it.

Question 4: Do All Religions Lead to God?

Research has shown that most Americans, including most Christians, believe that there is some truth in all the religions of the world. The fact is the Bible says that no religions lead to God. People don't go to heaven because they are religious. It's not about religion; it is about a relationship with Jesus Christ. Salvation is not about demographics or denominations. It's about the sacrifice of Christ at Calvary and whether or not you believe that what he did there is all that God required to pay the penalty for your sin.

But if a person is sincere, isn't that all that matters? Sincerity isn't the road to God; faith is, and not just any faith, but faith in the right person. "Believe in the Lord Jesus, and you will be saved, you and your household" (Acts 16:31).

> **78 percent of Americans say all religions have elements of truth.**
> —*U.S. News & World Report*, March 2002

Don't all roads lead to God? You don't believe that either. Do all roads in the United States lead to Chicago? Go ahead: get on Interstate 40 or Interstate 5 or even Interstate 95. See if you get to Chicago. Only the roads designed to take you to Chicago will actually get you there. God designed a road to himself. Jesus said, "I am the way, and the truth, and the life. No one comes to the Father except through me" (John 14:6).

Don't get lost on the back roads of religion. Read God's roadmap and you'll find your way to God. It's always been through his Son.

Question 5: Why Am I Here?

Why do you exist? Why are you here? Does your life have any meaning or value? You were created by God, and everything God creates has intrinsic value. Speaking of God, the book of Ecclesiastes says, "He has made everything beautiful in its time. Also, he has put eternity into man's heart" (Eccl. 3:11). A meaningful life is both beautiful and eternal but we can't relate to eternity until we learn to relate to the eternal God.

Some have said that we have a "God-shaped hole" in our heart and cannot be happy until he fills that hole. Author Stephen Evans says this hole is "the desire for eternal life, the desire for eternal meaning, and the desire for eternal love."[2] It's no coincidence that all three come only from God.

Meaning in life is not found in what we do, who we are, or who we know. It is found in our relationship with God because he is the giver of meaning. Meaning is never intrinsic; it always comes from someplace, a relationship with someone. That Someone is God.

To understand why you are here, consult the only Book written by the only One who can give you genuine meaning. The purpose of your life is to glorify God by connecting with him personally and connecting him personally to others (Matt. 28:6; John 1:41, 45; Eph. 2:8–10; Phil. 3:8–11). That will give your life meaning!

Question 6: Can God Ever Forgive Me?

If you're struggling with forgiveness today, you need to read the Bible. If you think you've done so many rotten things that God

---

[2] C. Stephen Evans, *Why Believe? Reason and Mystery as Pointers to God*, revised ed. Grand Rapids MI: Eerdmans, 1996), 58–60.

can't possibly forgive you, you really need to read the Bible. If God could forgive King David for sleeping with Bathsheba and then sending her husband to the front of the battle in order to be killed (2 Sam. 11:1–27), God can forgive you.

If you want God to forgive you, don't try to hide your sin. Admit it and confess it to God. "Whoever conceals his transgressions will not prosper, but he who confesses and forsakes them will obtain mercy" (Prov. 28:13). Confess and then forsake or leave it behind. "If we confess our sins, he is faithful and just to forgive us our sins and to cleanse us from all unrighteousness" (1 John 1:9). Bible illiteracy robs people of the joy of forgiveness and a whole lot more—all because they don't read the good news God has for them in his Word.

Question 7: What Happens After I Die?

The Bible records the story of the horrible crucifixion of Christ. You will remember it well if you saw the movie *The Passion of the Christ*. But God's Word also records that after three days in the grave, Jesus rose from the dead to live forever. He gave those who believe in him this promise: "Because I live, you also will live" (John 14:19).

Death is not the end; it's just a stopover on the way to eternal life. If you are flying to South America, you may well first fly to Miami. Miami isn't your final destination; it's just a stopover, a place to change planes en route to your final destination. Death is like that. It's not the end, it's where you change planes for eternity.

> **91 percent of Americans say reading the Bible has a great deal or somewhat "helped me find meaning in life."**
> —*The Gallup Poll*, December 1998

When you read God's Word you discover his promises. One of those promises is this: "'Death is swallowed up in victory. O death, where is your victory? O death, where is your sting?' The sting of death is sin, and the power of sin is the law. But thanks be to God, who gives us the victory through our Lord Jesus Christ" (1 Cor. 15:54–57).

Bible illiteracy robs you of answers you deserve. The answers are in the Bible, but they won't jump out of the book at you. You have to read the Word of God regularly to know the mind of God, the promises of God, the plan of God, the answers of God to life's key questions.

13

Bible Illiteracy
Hinders Spiritual Maturity

How long you've been a Christian only tells how long you've been on the road; it doesn't tell how far you've come.

—VANCE HAVNER

All of life is a journey along a continuum. We come into the world roaring like a lion and usually go out whimpering like a little puppy. We draw our first breath, and from that moment the clock starts ticking until our last. But in between the first and the last, we have the grand privilege of living.

Spiritual life is not much different from physical life. There's a point at which new life begins when you come to faith in Jesus Christ and another point at which you die in the Lord and go to be with him. But in between the first and the second, you have the grand privilege of living the Christian life.

Seeds That Sprout Need to Grow

How much did you weigh when you were born? How much do you weigh now? Okay, that's meddling, but the point is anything that is given life must grow.

American evangelicals surveyed don't believe reading the Bible is important for spiritual growth.

—The Bible Literacy Center, May 2006

God is so interested in you not remaining a spiritual infant that he has said much about how to grow his way. The psalmist reminds us that "The righteous flourish like the palm tree and grow like a cedar in Lebanon" (Ps. 92:12). Jesus also referenced growth in Mark 4:26–29 when he illustrated how the kingdom of God grows. First comes a tiny blade or sprout, then the budding head of the grain, and finally the full-blown head, which with other full-blown heads make the "amber waves of grain." The image is the progression from infant to adult.

Likewise the Master wanted us to appreciate that spiritual growth is both a gradual and continual process that begins with a sprout and ends with a harvest of full spiritual maturity. Even though a farmer may not fully understand the process of growth, still he plants seeds; they sprout and grow. You need not fully understand the process of how you grow spiritually, but you ought to see gradual and continual progress in moving down the road toward full spiritual maturity. If you're not, it's because of the great blight on spiritual growth today—Bible illiteracy. It's the major reason why spiritual seed that sprouts sometimes never produces much fruit.

A Very Good Place to Start

Do you remember the words of Maria von Trapp's song in *The Sound of Music*? "Let's start at the very beginning, a very good place to start." Well, in writing his friends to encourage them to grow once they had trusted Christ as Savior, the Apostle Peter noted that the beginning is also a very good place to start toward full spiritual maturity. Peter says, "Like newborn infants, long for the pure spiritual milk, that by it you may grow up to salvation" (1 Pet. 2:2).

As newborn babies crave milk, newborn believers are starving for the pure spiritual milk found only in God's Word. They can't grow without it. Immediate nourishment is needed for newborns to begin to grow.

> **America's spiritual confusion undoubtedly relates to the fact that most people own a Bible but few know what's in it.**
> —*The Barna Update*, December 22, 2003

But Peter's friends were not all newborn believers. Some of them had been in the faith ten or even twenty years. They were, however, still eating like "infants," depriving themselves of the adult food necessary to sustain their spiritual growth.

Today, too many Christians are at the same place spiritually they were the day they were saved. They're stuck in spiritual infancy. They've never grown. They're still spiritual babies. When it comes to eating the meat of the Word, they're more than content with baby food. Therefore, since Bible illiteracy keeps a lot of Christians stuck in spiritual infancy, these perpetual babies are not able to live as full-grown spiritual adults who should be feeding other spiritual infants. If you want to grow as God designed, you have to adopt a diet that is more in keeping with adults and less adapted to spiritual infants. So what will it take to move you from baby food to meat and potatoes?

Eat a Balanced Spiritual Diet

If a balanced diet is one of the keys to being healthy physically, why wouldn't it be one of the keys to being healthy spiritually? Eating a balanced diet means getting proper amounts of the five basic Bible food groups:

- History—books such as Genesis, Joshua, 1 Samuel, and Acts
- Prophecy—books such as Daniel, Revelation, Ezekiel, and Jeremiah
- Poetry—books such as Psalms, Proverbs, Ecclesiastes, and Song of Solomon
- Gospels—Matthew, Mark, Luke, and John
- Epistles—books such as Romans, Ephesians, 1 Peter, and Jude

You don't need to eat from these five groups every day, but if you want to establish good growth habits, you do need to eat repeatedly from all five. So what's for dinner today? Eat from the Law and the Prophets. Have a side salad from the Psalms. Devour the doctrine of the epistles, and enjoy the veggies of the Gospels. That's how to grow to spiritual maturity.

Green Beans or Gummi Bears

Unfortunately, a growing number of twenty-first-century Christians don't grow to maturity because they have developed a taste for spiritual junk food. Spiritual junk food isn't always bad; it's just not as good as a balanced, vitamin-enriched diet. Statistics prove that millions of evangelical Christians eat a steady diet of spiritual junk food. They crave the tasty, well-advertised, highly decorative side dishes and desserts but don't eat their vitamin-enriched lean meat and vegetables. A growing number of Christians want Gummi Bears; what they need is green beans.

> 24 percent of Americans say doctrines and beliefs are the most important part of religion.
>
> 69 percent say an individual's spiritual experience is the most important.
>
> —*Religion & Ethics Newsweekly,* March 2002

Gummi Bears are tasty, they're cute, they're squishy, they're brightly colored, they've got everything going for them—except nutritional value. On the other hand, green beans may not be as tasty, as cute, nor as flashy or brightly colored. The main thing green beans have going for them is that they're what you need. They'll build you up and make you strong and healthy. The diet of the twenty-first-century church consists of too many Gummi Bears and not enough of God's green beans. It's okay to eat an occasional Gummi Bear; just don't make it your meal every day.

When you buy Christian books, don't look for Gummi Bears. When you listen to Christian radio or watch Christian television, don't hone in on Gummi Bears. Don't let style rob you of substance.

Adopt God's diet so you will grow "to mature manhood, to the measure of the stature of the fullness of Christ, so that [you] may no longer be children" (Eph. 4:13–14). Gummi Bears make great snacks, but green beans make a life.

Don't Settle for Principles

One more thing: often we skim the Bible, looking for principles to live by. But there's a real danger in missing the substance of Scripture itself because we've settled for the principles of Scripture. Principles are good, but often they represent only the tops of the trees, whereas we need to be examining the roots and trunks as well as the tops.

Tyndale House Publishers commissioned a national survey called "Bible Reading in America." The survey discovered that 86 percent of American adults claimed to know the basic principles of the Bible "somewhat" or "very well," but a large percentage performed poorly on a basic quiz of Bible knowledge.[1] What does that tell you? It tells you that too many Christians only go to the Bible when looking for quick and direct answers rather than reading it consistently and discovering the answers as a result.

When you read God's Word, don't just skim the highlights to gain some how-to principles. That's not the way to take back the Book. Get down in there and mix it up with the words of Scripture themselves.

Confronting Satan's Strategy

Author and theologian J. I. Packer wrote in the foreword to R. C. Sproul's *Knowing Scripture*: "If I were the devil, one of my first aims would be to stop folks from digging into the Bible . . . I should do all I could to surround it with the spiritual equivalent of pits, thorn hedges, and man traps, to frighten people off."[2] That's exactly what Satan does. His strategy is clear. He puts thoughts in our mind

---

[1] Reported by John Wilson, "The Living Bible Reborn," *Christianity Today*, October 28, 1996, 35.
[2] J. I. Packer, "Foreword" in *Knowing Scripture*, R. C. Sproul (Downers Grove, IL: Tyndale, 1977).

such as: *There sits that Bible. It's big, thick, has a black cover. It's too difficult to read or understand. It was okay for my grandmother, but it doesn't have anything to say to me.*

> In our churches there is little emphasis on the importance of getting to know your Bible. Whatever else people do in between church services, they don't "soak" themselves in the Bible in order to get to know it well.
> —J. I. Packer

If those thoughts hit you when you see your Bible lying there on the table, you're not alone. Satan says it to all of us. None of it is true, of course, but if the devil can get you to believe it, he's already won. Satan's subtle strategy is to keep you from reading your Bible entirely or settling for too little when you do.

Why is Bible illiteracy so dangerous? Because life is a continuum and Bible illiteracy keeps us on the short end of the continuum. Jesus said, "I came that they may have life and have it abundantly" (John 10:10). When you come to Christ in faith, you have life, but to have the abundant life he spoke of, you must take care that Bible illiteracy doesn't perpetuate your spiritual infancy.

14

Bible Illiteracy Threatens Theological Integrity

I have watched with growing disbelief as the evangelical church has cheerfully plunged into astonishing theological illiteracy.

—DAVID WELLS

Not all Americans who lived during our founding decades were theologians. In fact, very few were. But most Americans were at least Bible literate in those years and thus knew a good deal about God and what we would call theology (what God reveals about himself, his purposes, plans, promises, etc.). But, with time, Bible illiteracy settled in across America like a thick cloud; and without the sunlight of God's Word, an everyday understanding of theology became rare indeed.

In this chapter, we want to explore how a lack of Bible knowledge has also contributed to a lack of theological savvy. Many Americans are theologically naïve today. That's not unreasonable or unexpected, but what is unreasonable and unexpected is the fact that many evangelical Christians are every bit as theologically naïve as people who don't even attend church.

Who's to say what's theologically correct? You? Me? Our peers? None of the above? How about God? He is. If the Bible is what it claims to be—a revelation of the mind of God to the minds of men— then God alone is in a position to determine what is truthful with regard to his character, his plans, and his purposes.

The Tyranny of the Affective

Is it really important whether what you believe is true or not? Isn't it most important what your beliefs mean to you—how they make you feel and act? Many people think so, but "the greatest enemy of biblical truth these days isn't any direct attack that denies that the Bible is true. The greatest enemy is the attitude that it just doesn't matter all that much whether a belief is true; what matters is how a belief makes you feel."[1]

For example, wouldn't you like to believe that God will save everyone from their sins simply because he is God and loves them? That just sounds so right. But that's not theological truth. The Bible teaches that the wages of sin is death and every person who sins will face death as a consequence of their sin (Rom. 6:23; Ezek. 18:4, 20). "Feel good" or not, that's what the Bible says.

When the affective domain (how we feel about things) overrules the cognitive domain (what we know about things), theological make-believe is the result. In other words, we make the Bible say anything we believe. We make up our own belief system. There's no greater threat than this to theological integrity.

Taking Stock of What We Believe

Not all Americans are as guilty of making up their own belief system as some. There is evidence that, for the most part, America still holds to many theological truths that are found in the Bible. For example, belief in some sort of life after death is held by 81 percent of Americans, although we're often fuzzy about what eternal life means.[2]

---

[1] *The Good Book*, October 6, 1996, www.backtogodhour.org/sermons/sermon_detail.cfm?ID=35489.
[2] The statistical data that follows is taken from *The Barna Update*, "Americans Describe Their Views about Life after Death," October 21, 2003.

> Approximately 76 percent of Americans believe that heaven exists, describing it as "a state of eternal existence in God's presence" (46%). Others (30%) said it's "an actual place of rest and reward where souls go after death." Another 14 percent say it is just symbolic.
>
> —*The Barna Update*, October 21, 2003

Americans are a bit more tenuous in their beliefs about hell than they are about heaven. Four out of ten adults believe that hell is "a state of eternal separation from God's presence" (39 percent), and one-third (32 percent) say it is "an actual place of torment and suffering where people's souls go after death." About 13 percent or one in eight adults believe that "hell is just a symbol of an unknown bad outcome after death."[3]

Interestingly, while hell is real in the minds of many Americans, most do not expect to go there. Just one-half of 1 percent expect that hell will be their final destination. Nearly two-thirds of Americans (64 percent) believe they will go to heaven.[4]

No Biblical Basis for Beliefs

While these numbers don't appear all that bad, there is a hidden snake in the grass. Even though most Americans believe in life after death, not everyone is entirely sure about their personal, ultimate destination. They believe they'll go to heaven, but they don't know why they believe that. They just "feel" they will.

> 43 percent of all Americans believe they will go to heaven because they have "accepted Jesus Christ as their Savior." 15 percent believe it's because "they have tried to obey the 10 Commandments." Another 15 percent said they will go because "they are basically good people." 6 percent believe God loves all people and will not let them perish.
>
> —*The Barna Update*, October 21, 2003

[3] Ibid.
[4] Ibid.

One in every four adults (24 percent) admitted that they have "no idea" what will happen after they die. Among those who expect to go to heaven, there were deep differences in how they expect to get there. Few have any idea of what the Bible says are heaven's entrance requirements.[5]

Contradictions Galore

George Barna, whose group conducted the research outlined above, noted "Americans' willingness to embrace beliefs that are logically contradictory." As shown, among born-again Christians who have personally trusted Jesus' death on the cross as payment for their sin, 50 percent contend that a person can earn salvation based upon good works.[6] That's astounding! This theological inconsistency indicates the degree to which even American Christians are willing to allow their feelings to guide their belief systems instead of God's Word.

The cause of the demise of theological understanding is primarily Bible illiteracy. We simply don't know our Bibles as well as we think we do. The lack of understanding basic theological concepts in Scripture has mounted a very serious threat to the theological integrity of the twenty-first-century church. However, what Christians believe down deep in their hearts and minds is not the only casualty of Bible illiteracy. How we view the world outside us and around us has also been impacted by our declining knowledge of the Bible.

Bible Illiteracy and the Death of a Christian Worldview

You would think that all Christians have a biblical view of the world around them. Yet the research says just the opposite. Most Christians do not have a biblical worldview.[7] According to Barna

---

[5] Ibid.
[6] Ibid.
[7] "Most Adults Feel Accepted by God, but Lack a Biblical Worldview," *The Barna Update*, August 9, 2005.

research, just 9 percent of all adults in America who claim to be "born again" have a biblical worldview. You didn't read that incorrectly—it was 9 percent.[8]

The Gallup Organization reports that 65 percent of Americans agree that the Bible "answers all or most of the basic questions of life." Yet, amazingly, 28 percent of Americans who believe the Bible "answers all or most of the basic questions of life" say they rarely or never read the Bible.[9] Therein lies the problem.

> In 2004, 16 percent of all adults agreed somewhat that the Bible is totally accurate in all of its teachings compared with 19 percent in 2002 and 25 percent in 1991. Still, 12 percent of born-again Christians disagree that the Bible is totally accurate in all its teaching.
>
> —*The Barna Update,* "The Bible"

Left without a biblical basis, many Christians don't know what to believe these days. They're mixed-up and confused. Their worldview is full of competing voices, and they're making decisions on the basis of how they feel.

But with more books about growing the church and more training in leadership skills, surely today's pastors are ready to meet the challenges presented by the death of theological integrity? Surely the pastor can instill a biblical worldview into his people and help lift them out of the quagmire of Bible illiteracy? You'd think.

Pastors Face a Personal Dilemma

Much of the research indicates pastors are often part of the problem. Isaiah 56:11 makes reference to "shepherds who have no understanding; they have all turned to their own way." It's important not to generalize here because I know many fine men of God who are concerned about their people's understanding of the Word. Still, based on

---

[8] *The Barna Update,*" January 12, 2004.
[9] *The Gallup Organization,* October 20, 2000.

interviews with 601 senior pastors nationwide, representing a random cross-section of Protestant churches, The Barna Group reports that only half of the country's Protestant pastors—51 percent—have a biblical worldview.[10]

George Barna argued, "The low percentage of Christians who have a biblical worldview is a direct reflection of the fact that half of our primary religious teachers and leaders (senior pastors) do not have one." In some denominations, the vast majority of clergy do not have a biblical worldview, and it shows up clearly in the data related to the theological views and moral choices of people who attend their churches."[11]

Follow the progression. We read our Bibles less and therefore understand less biblical truth. We attend a church where biblical truth was once the hallmark of the pulpit, but is no more and our "shepherd" isn't always sure how Christ would view the world. And what's the unintended result? Our personal Bible illiteracy threatens our personal theological integrity and we aren't even aware of it.

Bible Illiteracy and the Rise of Cult Activity

Cults thrive on people who have no answers for what they believe. Ignorance of what the Bible says and what it means has played a major role in making Christians of all stripes vulnerable to the teachings of the ever-more subtle, and I might add, ever-more numerous cults. When Paul told Timothy to pass on to another generation the body of truth that had been passed on to him, the apostle knew this was the only safeguard against theological deception (2 Tim. 2:2). When truth is handed down from godly parents, a godly pastor, a good mentor, or gracious grandparents, this is no guarantee that the theological inconsistencies of the cults will be clear, but it sure helps.

You all need to be aware of the tactics of the cults, if not for your

[10] *The Barna Group*, January 12, 2004.
[11] Ibid.

safety, then for the safety of your children or grandchildren. So beware of any person or group that:

- Insists that you read only their special version of the Bible
- Implies that all other versions are inaccurate or flat-out wrong
- Forbids you to discuss with your pastor or parents the study you're doing, suggesting that doing so will only cause you to doubt the truth
- Offers to "walk you through" a personal study in the Bible
- Tells you not to read the Bible for yourself, that without their help you'll only become confused.

The key to success for every cult is to keep you away from personal Bible study or from people who read and understand the Bible. The Bible is a cult killer. Bible illiteracy is a cult enabler. To preserve your personal theological integrity and to keep your family safe from cults, do whatever it takes to recover Bible literacy in your family. A right understanding of what the Bible says and means is critical to your belief system. The more quality time you spend with God in his Word the less chance you'll become a theological casualty.

15

Bible Illiteracy Causes
Moral Uncertainty

*We now live in a "post-Christian" America. The Bible has ceased to
be a common base of moral authority for judging whether something
is right or wrong, good or bad, acceptable or unacceptable.*

—ALAN CRIPPEN

It's not uncommon in our society for people to be at loose ends
morally. They don't know what's right or what's wrong. They don't
even know how to find out. There is a lot of moral uncertainty in
the world today. Do you wonder why?

In the last several presidential campaigns in the United States, the
theme of family values surfaced repeatedly. Everyone was for family values. The only problem was, no one seemed to be able to define
either word—*family* or *values*. The words meant something different to almost everyone. This is classic postmodernism.

We have difficulty getting a handle on what values are because
the word *value* is often used interchangeably with *virtue*, and that's
a mistake. They are not the same. It's like using the words lightning
and lightning bug interchangeably. One is a delightfully harmless
little flashing creature; the other is a powerful surge of hot energy
that can kill.

Values versus Virtues

According to Webster's Dictionary,[1] to *value* means to assign relative
worth or importance to something or someone. Therefore, values are

---

[1] *Webster's Ninth New Collegiate Dictionary.*

those things to which we assign worth based on how important they are to us. *Virtue* means a particular moral excellence that conforms to a standard of right. Morality was once based on virtue; now it is based on value. So we decide what is moral based on what we value or not. Virtue conforms to a standard of right; but now we are our own standard of right, and so *virtue* has slipped from our vocabulary and has been replaced by *value*.

The Hebrew people of the Bible understood virtue. The standard of right was God's Ten Commandments. Thus, Hebrew virtues were godliness, honor, fidelity, and truth. The ancient Greeks also understood virtue. The fundamental virtues celebrated by Aristotle were wisdom, justice, temperance, and courage. When Jesus came onto the world scene, he breathed new life into the Hebrew virtues and added a few of his own—faith, hope, and love. In each case, there was an objective standard upon which these virtues stood, whether it was the Pentateuch (the first five books in the Old Testament, which were written by Moses), the Greek ideal (mathematical perfection, goodness, justice, beauty, etc.), or the teachings of Christ (humility, purity, honesty, love, etc.).

> **Unprincipled men and women, disdainful of their moral heritage and skeptical of Truth itself, are destroying our civilization by weakening the very pillars upon which it rests.**
>
> —Chuck Colson

But with the decline of Bible literacy over the last few generations there has come a proportionate decline in objectivity. In our postmodern world, what you feel is right for you, is right. Objective virtues have gradually been replaced with subjective values. Objective standards of morality (based on virtues) have gradually been replaced with subjective standards of morality (based on values).

A Sense of Gravity and Authority

Professor Gertrude Himmelfarb, in her classic book entitled *The De-Moralization of Society*, says, "So long as morality was couched in the language of 'virtue,' it had a firm, resolute character. The older philosophers might argue about the source of virtues, the kinds and relative importance of virtues, the relation between moral and intellectual virtues or classical and religious ones or the bearing of private virtues upon public ones. . . . But for a particular people at a particular time, the word 'virtue' carried with it a sense of gravity and authority, as 'values' does not."[2]

When the Bible became viewed as something less than God's objective standard for morality, when it began to be read little and heeded less, society became less acquainted with the divine basis for morality. In our values-oriented society, the individual replaced God as the judge of what was moral, and the strength of objective virtue gave way to the weakness of subjective value.

In the Bible, good and evil were clearly distinguished, clearly understood. The anger of the Lord God was raised again and again at his people when they blurred the lines between what was objectively good and evil (see Exodus 32). But now, as philosopher and academic critic Allan Bloom says, "We have come back to the point where we began, where values take the place of good and evil."[3]

Virtues are objective; values are subjective. Virtues conform to a standard of right; values conform to the individual. In the Christian world, that standard of right is the Bible. The more unfamiliar with the Bible we become, the more unfamiliar with virtue we become. All we have left are values that change with the wind.

The Effects of a Virtueless Society

People robbed of virtue and convinced that they alone can determine what values are right for them suffer serious consequences as a result. In their book *13th Generation: Abort, Retry, Ignore, Fail?*

---

[2] Gertrude Himmelfarb, *The De-Moralization of Society* (New York: Alfred A. Knopf, 1994), 11.
[3] Allan Bloom, *The Closing of the American Mind* (New York: Simon and Schuster, 1987), 194.

Neil Howe and Bill Strauss show what happens when teens are not taught, and do not live by, objective standards of truth:

"They are two times more likely to try to physically hurt someone; two times more likely to watch a pornographic film; two times more likely to get drunk; two and one-quarter times more likely to steal; three times more likely to use illegal drugs; and six times more likely to attempt suicide, the number one cause of death among teens."[4]

To what can we compare a society that clings tenaciously to personal, subjective values and casts aside biblical virtues? Who would better know than the parents of students at Columbine High School in Littleton, Colorado? If ever there was a classic clash of values against virtues, that was it. When Eric Harris, aged eighteen, and Dylan Klebold, aged seventeen, taunted, tormented, and massacred twelve of their peers and a teacher (while seriously wounding twenty-three others), they were acting in concert with their own values. We were shocked when the news of the Columbine tragedy was first shown on television. But was shock the right reaction? Probably not. We created a world devoid of virtue, and now we are paying the price for our creation.

Standing for God in the Public Square

In 2003 the commonwealth of Massachusetts passed America's first same-sex marriage law. Often called "gay marriage," "gender-neutral marriage," or "equal marriage," these unions are recognized by the Netherlands, Belgium, Canada, and most recently Spain.[5]

> The level of biblical illiteracy among Christians may be one reason why many believers hesitate to stand for godly values on the public scene.
>
> —Fred Jackson and Bill Fancher

---

[4] Neil Howe and Bill Strauss, *13th Generation: Abort, Retry, Ignore, Fail?* (New York: Vintage Books, 1993).

[5] The controversial same-sex marriage legislation passed final reading in Canada's House of Commons, sailing through in a 158 to 133 vote. Supported by most members of the Liberal Party, the Bloc Québécois, and the NDP, the legislation passed easily in June 2005.

Given the clear teaching of the Bible and the equally clear divine con-demnation of same-sex marriages, you have to wonder why the Christian community was so slow in responding to the Massachusetts ruling. It went nearly unchallenged in debate before passing and was almost unchallenged for months afterward. Where was the evangeli-cal voice? Who was speaking for biblical morality? Hardly anyone.

One reason why the evangelical community was so slow in respond-ing to this groundbreaking state legislation is that we've become so bib-lically illiterate, we don't know what God says about homosexuality, lesbianism, or other forms of morally deviant behavior. Had the Christian public been better informed by the Bible, it would have been better pre-pared to respond to this challenge to God's plan for marriage.[6]

So, how did we get into the moral mess we are in today?

Americans Adrift in Moral Malaise

When The Barna Group surveyed Americans on their feelings about morality, two out of every three (65 percent) said they worried about the future of our nation. Three out of four adults (74 percent) said they were concerned about the moral condition of the United States. They should be.[7]

The reason why there is so much moral uncertainty in America today is that there's so much biblical illiteracy. If you don't know God's "take" on abortion, same-sex marriage, euthanasia, pornog-raphy, cloning, or any other moral or ethical issue, you are left with the "take" of the talk show host, the newspaper columnist, the uni-versity professor, or the television reporter.

> **54 percent of people surveyed have spent more than 5 hours watching TV in the last seven days.**
>
> —The Bible Literacy Center, May 18, 2006

---

[6] For reasons to oppose same-sex unions see "Eleven Arguments against Same-Sex Marriage" by Dr. James Dobson at Focus on the Family's web site Citizen Link, www.family.org/cforum/extras/a0032427.cfm.

[7] "Most Americans Are Concerned about the Nation's Moral Condition," *The Barna Update*, April 30, 2001.

More than half of the young adults (52 percent) and teenagers (54 percent) base their moral choices on feelings and beneficial outcomes. Just 7 percent of teenagers said their moral choices were based on biblical principles. Adults do a little better at 13 percent.[8]

As our understanding of the Bible decreases each year, we can expect to see a proportionate increase in silence from the born-again community. It's inevitable. The less we know of God's Word, the less vocal we become in taking a stand for God in the public square. America's moral condition in the twenty-first century is the direct result of America's Bible illiteracy. Until we address Bible illiteracy, we will make no progress in overcoming our poor moral condition.

---

[8] "Americans Are Most Likely to Base Truth on Feelings," *The Barna Update*, February 12, 2002.

16

Bible Illiteracy Weakens Our Defense of the Gospel

The greatest enemy of biblical truth these days isn't any direct attack which denies that the Bible is true. The greatest enemy is the attitude that it just doesn't matter all that much whether a belief is true.

—THE BACK TO GOD HOUR

What role does Bible illiteracy play in your ability to witness for your faith? It plays a big one. What impact does it have on your ability to defend what you believe? The impact is even bigger. The plague of Bible illiteracy creeping across America is weakening the Christian's ability to defend God's Word.

Apparently the Apostle Paul was not among those who were unwilling, or unable, to defend the gospel. From a Roman prison cell he told the Philippians that he was in prison for "the defense and confirmation of the gospel" (Phil. 1:7). Again in verse 16 the apostle said, "I am put here for the defense of the gospel."

The Discipline of Apologetics

Throughout the history of the Christian church, the need for a reasoned defense of our faith has been so great that a whole discipline has grown up around it called "apologetics," a systematic, argumentative discourse in defense of Jesus Christ and the Christian faith. More often than not, apologists are trained philosophers, people who have sharpened their ability to think, to reason, to be logical, and to be articulate in their defense of what they believe.[1] Some modern-day apologists are William Lane Craig, Norman Geisler, J. P. Moreland, Gary Habermas, Josh McDowell, Lee Strobel, Ravi Zacharias, and a growing list of others.

"But that's not me," you say. Maybe it's not. But if you are an intelligent Christian—if you've been consistently in the Word of God—you should be able to do on a personal level what those apologists do on a professional level.

The Goal of Apologetics

Apologetics is not designed to prove the Word of God, but to provide an intellectual basis for faith. The goal of apologetics is not to convince a person to become a Christian contrary to his will; rather, the objective is to place the facts of the gospel (the good news that Jesus Christ died for our sins) before men and women in an intelligent fashion so that, if drawn by the Holy Spirit, they can make a meaningful commitment to Jesus as Savior.

So what kind of knowledge is essential for a reasonable defense of what we believe? The kind of knowledge needed is knowledge of the Bible, the basis for what we believe.

> An intelligent Christian ought to be able to point up the flaws in a non-Christian position and to present facts and arguments which tell in favor of the gospel.
>
> —Clark Pinnock

Thus, all you have to do is know your Bible well enough to tell others what you believe and why. When you defend the Bible in that way, you are the kind of apologist described in the Bible. Done correctly, you leave the other person thinking rather than angry.

---

[1] Probe Ministries has an article titled "Defending the Faith—Christian Apologetics in a Non-Christian World," which is a summary of the 1995 Evangelical Theological Society annual meeting. It features papers by J. P. Moreland (*Defending the Faith Philosophically*), Gary Habermas (*Defending the Faith Historically*), Charles Thaxton (*Defending the Faith Scientifically*), and Thomas C. Oden (*Defending the Faith Theologically*).

The What and How of Defending the Gospel

Have you ever needed to defend your character? If so, you likely did it with a vengeance because you know the truth about yourself. You defend yourself from a position of knowledge, not ignorance; from a position of strength, not weakness.

That's how it's supposed to be with our faith. You and I defend what we believe because we know the truth. We know what we believe. But if Bible illiteracy sneaks into our lives, if we aren't consistently reading and internalizing the Word of God, when it comes time to defend it before a university professor ridiculing Christianity, we'll likely be silent. Bible illiteracy weakens our defense of the gospel.

Those who give a true defense of the gospel and do it in a biblical way are not relying on their brilliance, their strategy, their arguments, or their impeccable logic. They are relying on the Holy Spirit of God. And the substance of their defense is not philosophy, logic, science, or knowledge. The substance is the Bible. So the greatest roadblock keeping you and me from defending our faith is failing to know what's in our Bible. Bible illiteracy weakens our defense of the gospel.

Defending Your Faith as a Means of Evangelism

The bottom line of defending your faith has to be evangelism. If it's not, it's better to live your faith in silence than to destroy it with argument. Dr. Greg Bahnsen is a Christian apologist. He recognizes that Paul always argued for the faith (evangelism) and not just about the faith. Bahnsen says:

> Evangelism naturally brings one into apologetics. This indicates that apologetics is no mere matter of "intellectual jousting"; it is a serious matter of life and death—eternal life and death. The apologist who fails to take account of the evangelistic nature of his argumentation is both cruel and proud. Cruel because he over-

looks the deepest need of his opponent and proud because he is more concerned to demonstrate that he is no academic fool than to show how all glory belongs to the gracious God of all truth.[2]

> **Gospel truth seeks no corners, because it fears no trials.**
> —Matthew Henry

If your purpose in defending the Gospel is anything less than the loving and meaningful presentation of the good news to the person with whom you're engaged in debate, you've lost the highest purpose of apologetics.

The Challenge from Bible Illiteracy

First Peter 3:15 tells us "In your hearts regard Christ the Lord as holy, always being prepared to make a defense to anyone who asks you for a reason for the hope that is in you." Think about what that means—what it will take to explain and defend your faith in places like the university classroom. What will it take to convince your Muslim coworker that your faith is genuine and worthy of his consideration? How will you speak both truthfully and lovingly to your children who have come under the clutches of a cult? What is the key to reaching out in evangelism to your friends and family? The answer to all of these questions is the same. To be "prepared to make a defense to anyone who asks" requires a deepening degree of understanding of the Bible and its contents.

Bible illiteracy robs us of our ability to be effective communicators of truth. If we're unsure about what we believe, or unsure where to find answers in the Bible, why would we think we can convincingly defend our faith or share it with others? You are not the only loser when you leave your Bible unread. Those friends and family for whom you may be the only connection to God are the big losers. Bible illiteracy dramatically weakens your ability to share and defend the gospel and thus weakens your effectiveness as a follower of Christ. That's a price too high to pay without a fight.

---

[2] Dr. Greg Bahnsen, "Apologetics and Evangelism," www.cmfnow.com/articles/PA013.htm.

Part Six

Recovering Bible Literacy in America

The Bible has survived the attacks of its critics, but is struggling to survive the neglect of its friends.

—WOODROW KROLL

17

A Reason for
Hope

*I want to know one thing—the way to heaven . . . God himself
has condescended to teach the way . . . He hath written it down in
a book. O give me that book! At any price, give me the Book of
God.*

—JOHN WESLEY

**Casey Stengel, Satchel Paige, Billy Martin, Bob
Uecker**—baseball has had its characters over the years. None of
them is more unique than former New York Yankees catcher Yogi
Berra. The silver-tongued Berra is famous for his "Yogisms" such
as, "A nickel ain't worth a dime anymore" and "If you come to a
fork in the road, take it." My favorite Yogism is "It's déjà vu all
over again."[1]

That's how I feel about Bible illiteracy. We've been here before;
it's déjà vu. Bible illiteracy is back, but we beat it before. We can do
it again. When Bible illiteracy plagued God's people in the past,
many recognized the problem, took appropriate action, changed
their behavior, and came back stronger than ever. What others have
done in the past, we can do too. There is reason for hope. The demise
of Bible literacy in America is not too far gone that we can't do something about it, but we must hurry. If you think it can't be done, just
remember that God can do anything (Matt. 19:26) and he has given

---

[1] Two classic books containing "Yogisms" are: Yogi Berra and Dave Kaplan, *When You Come to
a Fork in the Road, Take It! Inspiration and Wisdom from One of Baseball's Greatest Heroes*
(New York: Hyperion, 2001) and Yogi Berra and Dave Kaplan, *What Time Is It? You Mean Now?
Advice for Life from the Zennest Master of Them All* (New York: Simon & Schuster, 2002).

victory before in the battle for Bible literacy. History can be a great teacher if we are good learners.

When the Bible Was Discovered in a Temple

Israel was the chosen people of God, but more often than not they didn't act like it. Sometimes God's people don't. Things weren't going so well in Jerusalem. Manasseh was both the longest reigning of Judah's kings and, regrettably, the most wicked. In addition to murder, among his sins listed in 2 Kings 21:2–9 are rebuilding the high places for pagan worship, encouraging the worship of Baal along with that of sun, moon, and stars, and burning his son as a child sacrifice.

Second Chronicles 33:11–16 says that sometime during his reign, Manasseh was taken as a prisoner of war to Babylon. While he was in captivity he genuinely repented, and God restored him as king. He then tried to abolish his former pagan practices but most of the people were already too far gone.

Manasseh died in 642 BC, at the age of sixty-seven, and his son Amon became king. But Amon had been deeply influenced by his father's early life and reverted to idolatry. Amon reigned just two years when he was assassinated. Amon's son Josiah, who was only eight years old, ascended to the throne. At this point Judah was in spiritual turmoil; her sin was deeply ingrained.

By age fifteen or sixteen, Josiah was already showing signs of devotion to God and discernment beyond his years. At age nineteen or twenty he began to take an interest in returning his nation to God. He removed the altars to the pagan gods erected by his father. Josiah began to reform and rebuild his own kingdom, religiously and politically, but the process was slow because the people were not as interested in reform as he was.

> **Bibles laid open, millions of surprises.**
> —George Herbert

Then something dramatic happened. In the eighteenth year of his reign, Josiah began rebuilding the temple, and Hilkiah the priest made a startling discovery. In some dusty unused holy cupboard, he found a copy of Torah, the Law of God. Hilkiah gave the old scroll to Shaphan the secretary, who rushed to the king and read it to him:

> Then Shaphan the secretary told the king, "Hilkiah the priest has given me a book." And Shaphan read from it before the king. And when the king heard the words of the Law, he tore his clothes. And the king commanded Hilkiah, Ahikam the son of Shaphan, Abdon the son of Micah, Shaphan the secretary, and Asaiah the king's servant, saying, "Go, inquire of the LORD for me and for those who are left in Israel and in Judah, concerning the words of the book that has been found. For great is the wrath of the LORD that is poured out on us, because our fathers have not kept the word of the LORD, to do according to all that is written in this book." (2 Chron. 34:18–21)

Neglected for years, the power of the Word on the king was dramatic. Josiah's early reforms now advanced exponentially.

Bible illiteracy was epidemic in the seventh century BC among the chosen people of God. They had so long neglected the Word that they had to blow the dust off of it when they found it. The same neglect is true of Americans too. But regardless of how neglected the Word becomes, there is hope. The secret to taking back the Book is simply to stop the neglect and start reading. That's exactly what Judah did and there was reformation in the land. If it can happen for them, it can happen for us.

When the Bible Was Discovered
in a Library

Martin Luther, the son of a Saxon miner, was born at Eisleben, Germany, on November 10, 1483. He entered the University of Erfurt when he was seventeen. After graduation he began to study law. However, while he was walking outdoors in the summer of 1505, a lightning bolt struck near him as he was returning to school. Terrified, he cried out, "Help! Saint Anna, I'll become a monk!" True to his word, Luther left law school and entered the Augustinian cloister in Erfurt on July 17, 1505.[2]

It was here that Luther happened on a Bible one day in the monastery library. His previous studies had left him quite unfamiliar with the Bible, so Luther began to read. He was taken prisoner by the Word of God; he couldn't get enough of it and read it enthusiastically. Luther encountered the living God in his Word and this not only changed the monk's life, but it also changed the landscape of Christendom.

> Surveys indicate that American evangelicals don't miss reading their Bible.
>
> —The Bible Literacy Center, May 18, 2006

The next year Martin Luther was sent to Wittenberg, where he continued his studies and lectured in moral philosophy. In 1511 he received his doctorate in theology and an appointment as professor of Scripture, which he held for the rest of his life.

Martin Luther was well acquainted with the scholastic theology of his day, but he made the study of the Bible, especially the epistles of Saint Paul, the center of his work. His studies led him to the conclusion that Christ alone is the mediator between God and man and that salvation comes by God's grace alone and is received

---

[2] To learn more of Luther's life, see: Roland H. Bainton, *Here I Stand: A Life of Martin Luther* (New York: Meridian, 1995) and Roland H. Bainton, *The Reformation of the Sixteenth Century* (Boston: Beacon Press, 1985).

by faith alone rather than by indulgences or any other work of man. His approach to theology soon led him into a clash with the Catholic Church he served, precipitating the dramatic events of the Reformation.

Luther's breakthrough in that Erfurt library was as simple as it was profound. Bible teacher and author John Piper summarizes:

> One of the great rediscoveries of the Reformation—especially of Martin Luther—was that the Word of God comes to us in a form of a Book. In other words Luther grasped this powerful fact: God preserves the experience of salvation and holiness from generation to generation by means of a Book of revelation, not a bishop in Rome, and not the ecstasies of Thomas Muenzer and the Zwickau prophets. The Word of God comes to us in a Book. That rediscovery shaped Luther and the Reformation.[3]

That's what we must rediscover in the twenty-first century if we are to call America back to the Bible. God has not been silent; he reveals himself in a Book—the Bible.

Bible illiteracy was rampant in fifteenth-century Germany. But what turned it around for those people is what will turn it around for us today. We must discover again that God comes to us in a Book— his Book, the only Book he ever wrote—and if we fail to read that Book, we fail to connect with God. We've turned it around before; we can do it again!

When the Bible Was Discovered in a Seminary

Founded in 1845, the Southern Baptist Convention (SBC), with over sixteen million members and more than 42,000 churches in the United States, is the largest Protestant denomination in the world. Today the SBC is by and large populated by those who deeply

---

[3] John Piper, "Luther Discovers the Book" from The Bethlehem Conference for Pastors, Bethlehem Baptist Church, Minneapolis, January 30, 1996.

appreciate the Bible and hold to the absolute truthfulness of Scripture, but it wasn't always so.

When Harold Lindsell wrote *The Battle for the Bible* in 1978, chapter 5 was dedicated exclusively to the Southern Baptist Convention and its seminaries.[4] Specifically targeted was The Southern Baptist Theological Seminary (SBTS) in Louisville, Kentucky. Given that SBTS is the flagship seminary of the SBC, and its oldest, Lindsell named names and cited specific examples of how unorthodox theology had been creeping into SBTS for decades and had become firmly entrenched.

In 1976 a student wrote a master's thesis at SBTS that seemed to prove the longer a student remained at the school, the less likely he was to believe in God's Word. The seminary president at the time had led the seminary deep into liberalism. During his tenure, numerous faculty questioned the validity of the Bible and guest lecturers outright attacked it. After serious allegations and a great deal of upheaval, the president retired in 1981. The trustees chose a replacement, and although he opposed the conservative resurgence that was taking place within the SBC at the time, he called for compromise and sought to move the school toward a conservative-liberal partnership. Unsuccessful at that, he resigned the presidency in 1992.

Then something truly amazing happened: SBTS rediscovered the Bible.

> **We cannot aspire toward God till we have begun to be displeased with ourselves.**
> —John Calvin

R. Albert Mohler Jr. was elected the ninth president of the school, one of the largest seminaries in the world. Dr. Mohler is an evangelical committed to the truth of God's Word and an articulate spokesman for that truth. He has been recognized both by *Time* and *Christianity Today* magazines as a leader among American evan-

---

[4] Harold Lindsell, *The Battle for the Bible* (Grand Rapids MI: Zondervan, 1978).

gelicals. In fact, *Time* magazine's web site called him the "reigning intellectual of the evangelical movement in the U.S."[5]

Al Mohler is a strong advocate for the Bible and, as I quickly discovered in visiting him, an ally in the battle for Bible literacy. God has used him to reshape Southern Baptist Theological Seminary into an institution "totally committed to the Bible as the Word of God."[6] The elevation of the belief in and study of God's Word at Southern in such a brief period of time is no less revolutionary than Luther's Reformation. And, it happened within our lifetime.

Just over a quarter of a century ago Bible illiteracy was epidemic in the Southern Baptist Convention and most especially in its seminaries. But the rediscovery of God's Word in SBTS and other SBC seminaries has meant that a whole new generation of expository preachers is being raised up to meet the Bible literacy needs of those 42,000 SBC churches.

As can be seen from the history of God's people, when we neglect God's Word, we revert to one form of paganism or another. But when we rediscover God's Word, we find new hope and direction for our lives. If you want to help call America back to the Bible, pray that God's people today will learn from the history of Josiah's day. Pray that twenty-first-century believers will join in a similar movement of God just as fifteenth-century believers did. Pray that the Bible—long neglected in our homes, our churches and our seminaries—will be rediscovered by courageous families, courageous pastors, courageous students, faculty, and administrators, and that a new reformation will dawn in us.

Bible illiteracy: we've been there before; but we don't have to live there again. Others before us have risen to the occasion and fought the battle. Now we must do the same.

[5] *Time.com*, April 15, 2003.
[6] See the mission statement of The Southern Baptist Theological Seminary at www.sbts.edu/aboutus/beliefs.php.

18

What Bible Literacy
Means to God

*The sacred page is not meant to be the end, but only the means toward
the end, which is knowing God Himself.*

—A. W. TOZER

Why do you read the Bible? And if you've struggled reading it, failed to keep at it time after time, why do you keep
trying?

"My mother tells me to."

"I feel guilty when I don't read the Bible."

"I'm looking for answers."

The reasons people give for reading, or at least attempting to
read, the Bible are many. I don't buy any of these reasons. I don't
think we are motivated to read the Word because of guilt; we handle guilt about other things with ease. We find answers in the opin-
ions of friends, newscasters, and radio talk show hosts. And as for
your mother telling you to, what other things does your mother tell
you that you don't do?

No, I believe we keep coming back to the Bible for one reason—to connect with the Author. We read the Bible because down
deep inside we believe God wrote it, and we want to touch him. It's
like the centerpiece of the Sistine Chapel, Michelangelo's *Creazione
Di Adamo*, where the great artist depicts the finger of God touch-
ing Adam's finger. Somehow we want to be touched by God and
to touch him and we believe that happens through reading his
Word.

Bible Literacy Is How God Fulfills Our Desire for Him

God is a personal being like you and me. He gets satisfaction when he accomplishes his goals the same way we do. One of God's goals is to make us supremely happy. He wants us to have joy and live lives that are absolutely fulfilled. And God knows that when you read your Bible, you blow the hatch on the channel he uses to satisfy one of the most basic needs we have—meaning.

The Man from Thagaste

Aurelius Augustine was born in AD 354 in Thagaste (modern Algeria), North Africa. He was gifted with a brilliant mind and enjoyed both academic success and the worldly pleasures at Carthage. But his life was a mess. Disappointed by Platonic philosophy and living in adultery, Augustine became restless in his hunt for truth and virtue. At age thirty-two, he found both in God through faith in Jesus Christ. Augustine said to the Almighty, "You have made us for Yourself and our hearts are restless until we find rest in You."

God knows when you fail to read his Word, you rob yourself of discovering real meaning in life by connecting with him. But when you read his Word, God is pleased because then he can accomplish one of his goals—to fulfill you in every sense of the word.

The Man from Clermont-Ferrand

Blaise Pascal was born June 19, 1623. A child prodigy, Pascal early became interested in the natural and applied sciences. He invented the first digital calculator. He was a mathematician, creating two new major fields of research in mathematics. But Pascal lived in the time when Copernicus's discovery that the earth moves around the sun made human beings appear insignificant in the larger order of things.

Facing the immensity of the universe, Pascal said, "The eternal silence of these infinite spaces terrifies me." Tormented by religious doubt, Pascal took seriously the question, Why are we here? His thoughts are revealed in his most famous book, *Pensees*:

> There once was in man a true happiness of which now remains to him only the mark and empty trace, which he in vain tries to fill from all his surroundings, seeking from things absent the help he does not obtain in things present. But these are all inadequate, because the infinite abyss can only be filled by an infinite and immutable object, that is to say, only by God Himself.[1]

Blaise Pascal discovered that only God can fill the big empty place in your life.

The God-Man from Heaven

How does one come to be filled by the "infinite and immutable object"? Jesus said, "No one knows who the Son is except the Father, or who the Father is except the Son and anyone to whom the Son chooses to reveal him" (Luke 10:22). When the Son of God reveals the Almighty God through the Word of God, "you will know the truth, and the truth will set you free" (John 8:32).

John Piper, in his now-classic book, *Desiring God,* says, "The pleasure Christian Hedonism seeks is the pleasure which is in God himself. He is the end of our search, not the means to some further end."[2] When you win the battle for Bible literacy in your own life, you not only discover the joy of God, you *are* the joy of God. He delights in our getting to know him, and the most direct way to make that happen is by reading what he has revealed about himself in his Word.

Bible Literacy Reads "Through" the Bible to the Author

When people tire of reading the Bible it's because they read it for the wrong reasons, or in the wrong way. They read their Bible to gain

---

[1] Blaise Pascal, *Pensees*, A. J. Krailsheimer, trans. (London: Penguin, 1966), 75.
[2] John Piper, *Desiring God* (Portland, OR: Multnomah, 1986), 18.

knowledge, store facts, or pick up a few principles to live by. Knowledge is good, facts are fun, and learning life principles is commendable, but if you get nothing more out of reading your Bible than these, it is no wonder you find it dry, stale, and easy to shove aside. There is a reason why you need to read through the Bible and discover the Author. When you see the Bible as a means to a dynamic relationship with God, you can't get enough of it because you can't get enough of him.

No Bibliolatry Allowed

If you stop at the Book and don't read through to the Author, you could be accused of worshipping a book. But serious Bible readers don't worship their Bible; they highly respect it, but they worship God.

Some have viewed the scribes and Pharisees as bibliolators. They did seem a bit stuffy about the Torah. But you have to give them this: they knew the Bible. When Herod asked the chief priests and scribes where Christ was to be born, these guys didn't have to go do research. They snapped back with the correct answer. But was the knowledge in their heads sufficient to change the sin in their hearts? No.

In an excellent article entitled "Is Bibliolatry Possible?" Steven M. Baugh astutely observes, "But it is a tragic fact that the scribes and Pharisees, though knowing the words of the Book, knew not its Author. 'You know neither me nor my Father,' pronounced Jesus. Perhaps it is bibliolatry to know the Book but not its Publisher. To know dead precepts, but not the living God. 'Thou shalt love the Bible thy Book with all thine heart, soul, and strength,' but God is expendable."[3]

Being Familiar with the Bible Is not Bibliolatry

Contrast the scribes and Pharisees, who knew the law but did not know the Lord, with Jesus who perfectly represented all that God wanted him to reveal. Think of the expressions Jesus used in responding to these Jewish religious leaders and others:

---

[3] Steven M. Baugh, "Is Bibliolatry Possible?" *Modern Reformation Magazine,* 5, no. 3 (May–June 1996).

"Have you not read what God said to you? . . . Isaiah was right when he prophesied about you hypocrites; as it is written. . . .What is written in the Law? How do you read it? . . . In your own Law it is written. . . . Have you not read in the book of Moses? . . . It is written in the Prophets."

> Nothing perhaps more strongly indicates the tone of a believer's spirituality, than the light in which the Scriptures are regarded by him.
> —Octavius Winslow

Jesus answered those who used the Good Book wrongly by means of the Good Book used rightly. He was familiar with what his Father had said, but was even more familiar with his Father. For Jesus, the Old Testament law was but a means to discover the eternal God. It was not a set of *dos* and *don'ts* but a way in which men and women could be fulfilled in God.

Bible Literacy Is How We Get to Know God

If we learn to read through the Bible to its Source, there is a wealth of discovery that can be made about God that cannot be found anywhere else. Even those statements in Scripture that undergird the uniqueness of the Bible are really a reflection on the Author more so than the writing.

God's Word Is What God Is

We say that the Bible is inerrant, and indeed it is. It is incapable of error in all that it teaches, not because of its copyists but because of its Author. If God is perfect in his essence and all his attributes, and the Bible is a revelation of the mind of God, if the Bible doesn't perfectly reflect his mind, it cannot be his Word (2 Tim. 3:16).

We say that the Bible is infallible and indeed it is. But that's not because of the character of Moses, David, Isaiah, Peter, or Paul. It's because of the character of God. By his nature, he cannot make a mistake, cannot reveal incorrect information, or cannot deny himself (2 Tim. 2:13). So if the Bible could contain mistakes, it couldn't be the Word of an infallible God.

We say that the Bible is eternal and indeed it is. "Forever, O LORD, your word is firmly fixed in the heavens" (Ps. 119:89). But the Bible isn't eternal because it has proven to be indestructible at the hands of those who have banned it, burned it, or betrayed it. It's the fact that it's God's Word that makes it eternal because God is eternal.

The Bible Reveals God on Paper

In the postmodern world you are presented with a religious menu. You can choose as your life guide the thoughts of Buddha, the teachings of the Koran, the tutoring of the Book of Mormon, or you can just let your heart lead you. You can climb the Andes and, as I saw someone do, sit cross-legged at some Inca holy site hoping to absorb the spiritual vibrations of the universe. You have a veritable smorgasbord of supposed options to connect with God. With so many options, is it possible that there might be one book that reveals God on paper?

> Some see the Bible as just one more ancient volume assembled from the ramblings of assorted desert poets. Those holding this view would be little short of insane to regulate their lives according to the primitive views of a bunch of early nomads," says Rabbi Daniel Lapin. "Pulling from the other end of the rope are those of us, both Jewish and Christian, who see the Bible to be nothing less than God speaking to humanity. From our perspective, it would be just as insane to ignore the Bible.[4]

> When American evangelicals were asked in which faith dimension they were strongest, 61 percent said "worship"; in which dimension would they most like to improve, "knowledge of the Bible."
> —*The Barna Update*, June 14, 2005

---

[4] Rabbi Daniel Lapin, *America's Real War* (Sisters, OR: Multnomah, 1999), 178.

If you believe God has spoken and what he said is written in the pages of his Word, it's not irresponsible to ignore reading the Bible. It's insane.

Bible Literacy Is the Ultimate Act of Worship

Worship comes from an old Anglo-Saxon word *worthscipe*. It means "to ascribe worth to." To worship God means to love him so deeply you find significant ways to demonstrate that he alone is worthy.

In the late twentieth century, worship became associated with singing. Singing, of course, can be an act of worship, but it is worship in its most minimal form. Singing takes little effort, requires no preparation, and reflects so little of the vastness of God's character and his plan that it excludes more than it reveals.

Reading God's Word Ascribes Worth to the Almighty

Reading God's Word, however, is the ultimate act of worship. It's important to God, "For You have magnified Your word above all Your name" (Ps. 138:2 NKJV). This was certainly true for Ezra and the Israelites:

> All the people gathered as one man into the square before the Water Gate. And they told Ezra the scribe to bring the Book of the Law of Moses that the LORD had commanded Israel. . . . And he read from it. . . . And the ears of all the people were attentive to the Book of the Law. And Ezra the scribe stood on a wooden platform that they had made for the purpose. . . . And Ezra blessed the LORD, the great God, and all the people answered, "Amen, Amen," lifting up their hands. And they bowed their heads and worshiped the LORD with their faces to the ground. . . .They read from the book, from the Law of God, clearly, and they gave the sense, so that the people understood the reading. (Neh. 8:1, 3–4, 6, 8)

Notice the elements of this worship service:

- The people gathered together in unity.
- They were in the public square.
- Ezra read publicly from God's Word.
- The people listened attentively as Ezra read.
- Ezra stood on a raised platform to read the Word.
- Ezra blessed or praised the Lord.
- The people vocalized and gestured agreement.
- The people all bowed to the ground in worship.
- The Bible was read clearly and distinctly.
- The meaning of the text was explained.
- All the people understood the Word.

How many of these elements are featured in your church's worship service today?

Reading the Bible was also much a part of the New Testament church (Acts 15:12–21, 30–35; 2 Cor. 1:13; Eph. 3:4; Col. 4:16; 1 Thess. 5:27). Reading Torah is still a part of the synagogue service in Judaism today. There are only some in the twenty-first-century church who have abandoned the reading of God's Word as part of their worship service.

Reading God's Word Pleases the Author

As a part of my responsibilities with *Back to the Bible*, I am given the honor of both a writing ministry and a radio ministry. I have authored more than fifty books. Speaking as an author, I can tell you that the greatest compliment you can give to me is to say, "I read your book." The ultimate pleasure for any author is to know that someone read what they wrote. May I remind you, God wrote a book. And he wrote only one. What do you plan to say to him should he ask you at the judgment seat of Christ, "Did you read my book?" Give that some thought, because you cannot snooker God the way you do your friends.

> Surveys indicate that American evangelicals rarely have a specific time, place or plan to study their Bible.
> —The Bible Literacy Center, May 18, 2006

The psalmist says of the words of the Lord, "More to be desired are they than gold, even much fine gold" (Ps. 19:10). So how much of your day do you spend working for man just so you can have your gold? Do you grab for your Bible as eagerly as you grab for the gold? When you desire God's Word more than you desire gold, even much gold—in fact, much pure gold—you please the Author of the Bible. If you don't take back the Book in your life and read it consistently, you are saying to its Author, "I don't care enough about you or your Book to read it."

That's what Bible literacy means to God. It means you love him, and you show it. It means you worship him, and you show it. It means you thirst for him, and you show it. Isn't it time we did some serious thinking about just how Bible-literate we are? Isn't it time for you to do some thinking?

19

We Can Recover

Turning things around will take a massive concerted long-term effort.
But we must try. We must pray for God's guidance and power to
bring about the reformation He undoubtedly desires for America.

—GEORGE BARNA

Apollo 13 was an American space mission, part of the Apollo program. It was intended to be the third mission to land on the moon. Instead, it became a drama for the ages. On April 14, 1970, 321,860 kilometers from earth, Apollo 13 commander Jim Lovell and crew members John Swigert and Fred Haise knew something was terribly wrong. When some Teflon insulation covering electric wires caught fire, it caused their number-two oxygen tank to explode.

Command module pilot Jack Swigert said, "Houston, we've had a problem here." Capsule Communicator's (CapCom's) Jack Lousma at the Houston Space Center replied, "This is Houston. Say again please."

Commander Jim Lovell repeated, "Houston, we've had a problem."

The race to save the lives of three American astronauts was on. The command service module had to be completely shut down. The planned lunar landing was scrubbed and an ingenious rescue plan was devised. After a single pass around the moon, the crew would survive by using their lunar module as a lifeboat.[1]

The Apollo 13 near-tragedy has lessons for all of us. What

---

[1] To learn more about Apollo 13 and the recovery of three American astronauts, go to: nssdc.gsfc.nasa.gov/planetary/lunar/apollo13info.html.

National Aeronautics and Space Agency (NASA) did to solve their problem can be instructive in winning the battle for Bible literacy. Here are four issues we must wrestle with if we are to stop the spread of Bible illiteracy in America.

Issue 1: Recognize That We Have a Problem

When Swigert and Lovell said, "Houston, we've had a problem," both the image and the integrity of the space program were immediately on the line. Denying that a problem existed may have preserved the image of the agency, but it also would have doomed the three astronauts. Instead, NASA acted with integrity, which demanded admitting they had a problem.

Denial is an attempt to reject unacceptable facts, situations, feelings, and thoughts in order to protect ourselves temporarily from things we don't want to know, things we don't want to think about, or things we don't want to feel. Those in the evangelical community battle the subtleties of denial as much as anyone. But to say that the evangelical church is in denial about the existence of Bible illiteracy is an understatement.

Most evangelicals—pastors and lay people—haven't even thought much about the problem. And when confronted with the reality of Bible illiteracy in their churches, most are prone to deny the problem exists. As long as the programs are progressing, income is steady, and the pews are full, most evangelicals smile broadly with a sense of success. But the combustible weakness of the church quietly awaits ignition. Like NASA, if we are going to fix the problem, we must first be honest enough to admit that it exists. Delay is not the answer. Integrity is.

Issue 2: Get Serious about the Problem

There is always peril in meeting a wise and subtle enemy in battle. An even greater peril threatens us if we don't take that enemy seriously. Sometimes in our fight with Satan, we are as much changed by him as the world is changed by us. The church in the twenty-first century does not always engage postmodernism; sometimes it is engaged by it. In our fight for the truth, sometimes truth becomes the first casualty.

> **Christians who lack biblical knowledge are the products of churches that marginalize biblical knowledge.**
> —R. Albert Mohler Jr.

Postmodernism is so pervasive in our society that it is foolish to believe the Christian or the church has escaped its influence. Most of us spend our weekdays in a postmodern world and it's almost impossible to leave its effects at the door when we enter the sanctuary. That's just what Satan wants. If he can make the Bible a stranger to our pulpits and induce us to relegate God's truth to a place of unimportance, he knows we don't have to deny the Bible. In effect, we already have denied it by marginalizing its influence in our lives. We don't take the problem seriously because at this point we don't even know what we don't know.

The brain trust at NASA not only admitted it had a problem with Apollo 13, but it also immediately threw its entire resources into finding a solution. NASA got serious, and as a result, three astronauts' lives were spared. If we are to win the battle for Bible literacy, we will have to get serious about this problem too.

Issue 3: Don't Fix Blame—Fix the Problem

So whose fault is Bible illiteracy in America? Does the blame lie in government, society, the church, the family, the individual? How about all of the above? A decade ago, the quarterly journal *O Theophilus*, published by The Center for Biblical Literacy, contained an interview with theologian J. I. Packer about the growing problem of Bible illiteracy in the church. *O Theophilus* asked, "Where would you put the blame for this problem? Is it in the ministry, the seminaries, the congregation?" Packer responded:

> I hesitate to allocate the blame specifically on one group alone. But I would start by saying Christian parents simply haven't stressed to

their children the importance of the Bible being their favorite book. That's where it starts.

Then, in the churches I'd blame pastors who are not stressing the fact that if you are to be a Christian, you should, as I like to say, have the Bible "running out of your ears." Most people only read a certain number of verses for some devotional thoughts, not to know what the book is actually saying.

And then I'd blame modern culture which aggressively distracts the people from becoming really literate in anything, not just the Bible. It is partly due to modern life being filled with so many things, you know, but also the attitude that you can get by in this world with only a smattering of knowledge about anything. As Christians, we are to be different than the world around us. In particular, we are to attain a fuller knowledge of the Word of God, whereas the world around us hasn't got a fuller knowledge of anything.[2]

> **Research confirms that the majority of laypeople do not study the Bible regularly. Christians simply don't take time to read and understand Scripture.**
> —Daniel Foster

So the answer to my initial question is, we're all to blame. But identifying who's to blame for the plague of Bible illiteracy doesn't really accomplish anything. What we must do is admit we have a problem, get serious about it, and be creative in fixing it.

Issue 4: Expect Behavioral Change

After the explosion onboard Apollo 13, there was serious scrambling among the scientists at the Johnson Space Center. Then came the assessment from NASA's scientists. Jack Lousma said something like, "We figure we've got about [fifteen] minutes worth of power left in the Command Module. So we want you to start getting over in the Lunar Module and getting some power on that."

---

[2] *O Theophilus*, III, no. 1 (Spring 1995).

Three days from home, the spacecraft had electricity for only fifteen minutes under normal circumstances. When the loss of power is so dramatic and life-threatening, things have to change. I believe the plague of Bible illiteracy has caused Christians to face a similar loss of power in their lives and mission. Without the power of the living Word saturating their lives, evangelical Christians of the twenty-first century are no less adrift than Apollo 13. Both need a plan for recovery.

> **How often would people need to read or listen to the Bible before they were satisfied?**
>
> • 29%—once a day or more often;
>
> • 40%—once a week or more often, but less often than once a day;
>
> • 12%—once a month or more often, but less often than once a week;
>
> • 19%—less often than once a month.
>   —Yankelovich marketing and advocacy study, January 13, 2006

Since there is no one-size-fits-all action plan for winning the battle for Bible literacy, in the chapters that follow we will focus on what we all can do to help the cause. One thing is sure—we won't win this battle with new programs, new resources, new buildings, or new ministries. Winning this battle will require new behavior.

Author of *The Message*, a contemporary-language Bible, Eugene Peterson says, "We talk of 'making the Bible relevant to the world,' as if the world is the fundamental reality and the Bible something that is going to help it or fix it. We talk of 'fitting the Bible into our lives' or 'making room in our day for the Bible,' as if the Bible is something that we can add on to or squeeze into our already full lives."[3] But if we're going to win this battle, all of that has to change.

Bible illiteracy has spread through the church like wildfire

---

[3] Eugene Peterson, *Eat This Book*. (Grand Rapids: Eerdmans, 2006), 67.

because God became an add-on and the Bible a minimal reference point in our lives. It's time to say *no more*. There is a national emergency, and we have to treat it as such. The very way we live our lives, our daily patterns of behavior, has to change dramatically if we're going to recover Bible literacy.

The Apollo 13 mission ended amazingly well. When the lunar module splashed down on April 17 of that year, the world watching by television breathed a collective sigh of relief. Let's pray that the battle to take back the Book also ends amazingly well.

20

What You Can Do

You all have by you a large treasure of divine knowledge, in that you
have the Bible in your hands; therefore be not contented in possessing
but little of this treasure.

—JONATHAN EDWARDS

The person in the best position to stamp Bible illiteracy out
of your life is you. The desire to address your own Bible illiteracy,
however, must come from deep within. David said, "The rules of
the LORD are true, and righteous altogether. More to be desired are
they than gold, even much fine gold" (Ps. 19:9–10). That desire
will encourage you to do something to win this battle.

History has shown us that wars are won one battle at a time.
That's how the battle for Bible literacy will be won too. It starts
with you winning your battle. In this chapter we'll explore how
you can read the Bible to win. Below are seven specific ways you
can improve your personal Bible literacy.

Read the Bible—Tithe Your Free Time to God

First, you've got to be convinced that you can do it, and that you
have the time to do it. In the Old Testament, each year the Israelites
were to give back to God a tenth of their produce, their wine, their
flocks, everything God provided them (Deut. 14:22–23). This was
referred to as a tithe. While in the New Testament we're only
instructed to give to the Lord liberally and cheerfully (2 Cor. 9:7), the
tithe is often seen as a minimum standard or guideline in giving to
God. While most evangelicals skimp on their tithe to God, at least

we understand the concept.[1] We typically think of tithing in monetary terms, but have you ever thought about tithing your time? Suppose you spent 10 percent of your day with God? What would that mean?

Mathematically, there are twenty-four hours in a day, which equals 1440 minutes. If you gave the Lord 10 percent of that time, he would receive 144 minutes every day. That's over two hours. Is that how much time you spend in reading the Word and in prayer now? Probably not.

But let's be fair. You have to work and sleep each for eight hours. You can't really tithe that time. So we're really talking about tithing in terms of your third eight-hour period in the day. That's 480 minutes, and a tithe of 480 minutes is forty-eight minutes daily.

If you gave God forty-eight minutes daily, you'd be giving him one-tenth of one-third of your day. Does that sound reasonable? But how are you going to find forty-eight minutes in a day? You start here: Instead of tacking God onto your schedule *where you can*, instead of watching your third reality show of the night, turn off the television, shut out everything else, and spend forty-eight quality minutes with God. If you do that, you could actually read the Bible through four times in one year—pretty amazing!

Read the Bible—Be Transformed, Not Just Informed

People often fail to read their Bible because they're reading God's Word for the wrong reasons. They read simply because they want to be informed. Instead, God wants them to read so they'll be transformed. Reading the Bible changes your life; it doesn't just explain it. That's true of no other book.

When an Ethiopian eunuch was reading from the scroll of Isaiah, and Philip asked if he understood what he was reading, the man said he did not. So Philip began with that very passage of Scripture

---

[1] One out of every six born-again Christians (16 percent) gives no money to his or her church. The proportion who tithed to their church was just 8 percent. "Evangelicals Are the Most Generous Givers, but Fewer than 10 percent of Born-Again Christians Give 10 percent to Their Church," *The Barna Update*, April 5, 2002.

and explained to him the good news about salvation through Jesus Christ (Acts 8:35). The result was the transformation of the eunuch's life.

John Wesley grew up in a pastor's home. He was ordained by the church and even went to the American colony of Georgia to convert the Indians. But Wesley was unconverted himself. A failure in America, he returned to England where he attended a Moravian meeting. What followed is described in this famous entry in John Wesley's journal:

> In the evening I went very unwillingly to a society in Aldersgate Street, where one was reading Luther's preface to the Epistle to the Romans. About a quarter before nine, while he was describing the change which God works in the heart through faith in Christ, I felt my heart strangely warmed. I felt I did trust in Christ, Christ alone for salvation; and an assurance was given to me that He had taken away my sins, even mine, and saved me from the law of sin and death.[2]

Prior to this night, John Wesley had read the Bible for information. But on this night he was transformed. From that point on, he would only read the Bible for ongoing transformation in his life.

> **If the book we are reading does not wake us, as with a fist hammering on our skull, why then do we read it?**
> —Franz Kafka

What we need from the Bible is not primarily information—God telling us things about himself and his world. Reading the Bible is all about transformation—God changing us from the inside out so we have an impact on our world. Read your Bible to become more of what God wants you to be. If you approach your Bible as a transformational tool you'll be transformed every time you read it.

---

[2] Wesley, John. *The Heart of John Wesley's Journal* (New York: Revel, 1903), 48.

Read the Bible—Metabolize the Word

Reading for devotional thoughts isn't enough. Reading for facts isn't enough. In fact, reading the Bible isn't enough. Perhaps Bible illiteracy has taken such strong root in all of us because we haven't allowed the Word to be absorbed (metabolized) into our spiritual system.

That may sound a bit odd, but it's thoroughly biblical. Ezekiel the prophet was given a book and commanded by God to eat it. "Son of man, eat whatever you find here. Eat this scroll, and go, speak to the house of Israel" (Ezek. 3:1). His contemporary Jeremiah was similarly instructed: "Your words were found, and I ate them, and your words became to me a joy and the delight of my heart, for I am called by your name, O LORD, God of hosts" (Jer. 15:16). And the apostle-prophet John also was told to eat the Book of God. "So I went to the angel and told him to give me the little scroll. And he said to me, 'Take and eat it; it will make your stomach bitter, but in your mouth it will be sweet as honey.' And I took the little scroll from the hand of the angel and ate it. It was sweet as honey in my mouth, but when I had eaten it my stomach was made bitter" (Rev. 10:9–10).

In each case, before the prophets could be of service to God, they were instructed to eat the Book. After devouring the Book, they were ready to speak for God. These three men were doing more than just reading the Word. They took the Word into their souls, down to their nerve endings, their muscles, their minds, and their imaginations. They made it part of their thinking process. They based their decisions and lived their lives on what they had absorbed into their spiritual system.

If we read God's Word today and don't think about it, pray it back to him, internalize it, or memorize it, we're just chewing on those precious words and spitting them out. We need to metabolize God's Word so it becomes a part of how we think, how we respond, what we say—in short, who we are.

Read the Bible—Chart Your Spiritual Growth

Every time you read God's Word and discover something new, write it down. Keep a journal of your spiritual walk. This is just to help you establish some markers along the road. That's how a journal charts your spiritual growth.

I don't keep a personal journal, but my markers are in my old Bibles. I have copies of God's Word that go back to my teen years. When I look at the notes or questions I've written in the margin, I often say, "Well, duh, everybody knows that." But back then, I was just learning it, so the notes I wrote in the margins of my Bible act as spiritual mileposts for me.

> I conceive that we can scarcely be engaged in any service more useful than in endeavoring to facilitate and deepen the study of the Bible.
> —D. L. Moody

Have you ever thought of writing your own commentary on the Bible? Why not? You can do it just as the experts can. Yours may not be as scholarly as theirs, but it will be yours. Don't worry about what you write. Just write it from what you have gleaned from reading God's Word, and it will help the theology of the Bible stick in your mind.

And what about a list of interesting data or facts you discover from reading your Bible? I do that. When I want to find an interesting name in the Bible, I go to my list of interesting names.[3] When I want to find a verse that says God is the creator, I don't go to a theology text. I go to my personal list of verses that indicate God created everything. What makes this list so much better than the theology textbooks or Bible dictionaries I own? It's mine! Get in the habit of writing while you read or immediately after, and you'll

---

[3] Some of my favorite Bible names are: Uz and Buz (Gen. 22:21); Zaphenath-paneah (Gen. 41:45); Kibroth-hattaavah (Num. 11:34); Zamzummim (Deut. 2:20); Ishbi-benob (2 Sam. 21:16); So (2 Kings 17:4); Koz (1 Chron. 4:8); Buz and Guni (1 Chron. 5:14–15); Shuppim and Huppim (1 Chron. 7:12); Mushi and Beno (1 Chron. 24:26); Jaala (Neh. 7:58); Bunni (Neh. 9:4); Jemimah (Job 42:14); and Maher-Shalal-hashbaz (Isa. 8:1).

be surprised how much you'll be drawn back to reading God's Word the next time just to make more discoveries.

Read the Bible for God's Purposes, Not Just Yours

Typically we read our Bibles for our own purposes. We come to God's Holy Word looking for answers, looking for promises, looking for principles, looking for direction, when we should come looking for God.

In *An Experiment in Criticism*, the last book C. S. Lewis wrote, he talked about two kinds of reading—the reading in which we use the Book for our own purposes and the reading in which we receive God's purposes for writing the Book.[4] Reading for our own purposes often deters us from ever reading the Bible again. But reading for God's purposes keeps us coming back daily.

Let's be honest. We read the Bible for what we can get out of it. We look for our favorite passages, our favorite promises, and we go back to our favorite stories time after time. As we noted earlier, when the Apostle John was told by the angel to eat the book, the angels warned, "It will make your stomach bitter, but in your mouth it will be sweet as honey" (Rev. 10:9). John ate to get the full benefit of what God intended, not to select the honey-covered benefits he craved.

Reading with your own agenda robs you from discovering God's agenda in the Bible. Initially it may give you a high, but it won't keep you coming back for more. The next time you read your Bible, set aside every expectation you bring to your reading. Don't look for the biblical text to flatter you, to please you, or solely to interest you. Instead, enter the text to meet God and let him reveal himself and his agenda to you. Tomorrow you'll be back for more because the Bible has more to offer you than you can handle.

---

[4] C. S. Lewis, *An Experiment in Criticism* (Cambridge: Cambridge University Press, 1961), 88.

Read the Bible—Be Enthusiastic

I'm amazed at how some people can make the most exciting things seem so dull, like reading a book while you're riding a rollercoaster. You miss the whole point if you don't participate passionately in the ride. People often read the Bible like that. They don't participate passionately in what they read. No wonder they don't enjoy it.

I believe God wants us to read his Word enthusiastically and with passion. King David provides us with a great example of this. Everything he did, he did with gusto, whether killing a lion, a bear, or a giant. David lived large, loved large, and sometimes sinned large. But when he read God's Word, he read large. David said, "Then my soul will rejoice in the LORD, exulting in his salvation. All my bones shall say, 'O LORD, who is like you, delivering the poor from him who is too strong for him, the poor and needy from him who robs him?'" (Ps. 35:9–10).

Perhaps you've seen those Hasidic Jews in their black hats and black coats praying at the Western Wall in Jerusalem. They don't stand still as they read the Torah; they bob and weave, sway and swat. And why? Because David said, "All my bones shall say, 'O LORD, who is like you?'" They want to read the Word with vigor, with their whole being.

If you've ever watched Yitzak Perlman at a concert, you know what I mean. This incredibly gifted violinist was crippled by polio, and yet after he limps on stage and sits in his chair, picks up his violin, and begins to play, no one remembers the braces on his leg. He devotes himself completely to his violin. Not only is his playing technically spectacular, but his energy, his enthusiasm for the piece he is performing, his physical jerks and gyrations all indicate that he is fully involved with his music.

Maybe we're missing too much when we read our Bible because we aren't fully involved in the Word when we read. Try this. When you read your Bible shut everything else out. Close the door. Turn off your radio. Concentrate solely on the text in front of you. Get into it the way Perlman gets into his music. Get into it the way the Hasidic

Jews get into reading and praying before the Western Wall in Jerusalem. Read to connect with God and for no other reason.

Scripture becomes dull because we make it dull. You can change that. Reading God's Word doesn't have to be stiff, formal, and uninteresting. Read as David did with all your bones, saying, "O LORD, who is like you?" Read aloud. Stand and read; sit and read; walk and read. Bottom line—the more you get into it, the more you'll get out of it.

Read the Bible—Make It Personal

The Bible is about God, not about you. But when you read your Bible, you'll find it much more meaningful if you keep looking for yourself in the text. In other words, make it personal. Reading the Bible to encounter God there is an interactive exercise. We have to participate; we need constantly to be asking questions; we must continuously be looking for ourselves. We do that by asking, "How would I respond to that?" or "What do I think about that?" or "If that were me, what would I do?" That's looking for yourself when you read your Bible.

> 90 percent of Americans say reading the Bible has a great deal or somewhat helped them to be more open and honest about themselves.
> —*The Gallup Poll*, December 1998

When the disciples were discussing what people were saying about Jesus at Caesarea Philippi, Jesus pointedly asked, "But who do you say that I am?" (Matt. 16:15). He demanded participation. What's your answer? What do you think?

When the chief priests' assistants were sent to Jesus to try to catch him saying something incriminating, they asked, "Is it right for us to pay taxes to Caesar or not?" Jesus demanded they produce a coin, the Roman silver denarius, and then asked, "Whose likeness and inscription does it have?" (Luke 20:24). He demanded participation. What's your answer? Where do you stand on this issue?

Helmut Thielicke, the German theologian, used to tell his students that they should read the Word to find themselves in it. To illustrate what he meant, he would tell them of his young son who, when just a tiny baby, Thielicke would hold in front of a mirror. When the baby would wave his arms, the reflection waved. When he kicked his feet, his reflection kicked. Suddenly the boy's face lit up when he realized *that's me!*

That's when the Bible lights up our face too—when we realize that we aren't just reading stories or history or parables. We are reading about ourselves. It's only when we get to a "that's me!" understanding of God's Word that we have truly understood the Bible.

Making the Connection

Too often we think the Bible dull or boring and claim it never says anything to us. But in reality we've simply failed to look for ourselves in the text. When we do, the Bible speaks volumes to us about how we should live our lives. When you read your Bible, don't spend so much time on the *wheres* and *whys* of the text. Spend more time connecting with the *Who* of the text.

Literary critic Denis Donoghue once commented that when the poet William Carlos Williams "saw a footprint he had no interest in the meaning of the experience as knowledge, perception, vision, or even truth; he just wanted to find the foot."[5] We can recover Bible literacy in America if we begin to connect with the One whose footprint is left in the Bible. When you find the foot and participate in what God reveals in his Word, reading the Bible will be the consuming joy of your life.

Taking Action

Okay, so you want to read your Bible but don't know where to begin. Maybe I can help. Depending on where you are with your Bible reading, to give you some incentive, here are several options

---

[5] Denis Donoghue, *The Ordinary Universe* (New York: Macmillan, 1968), 182.

you can use to get into God's Word right away. I call them challenges because I am passionate about you taking your Bible reading to the next level—wherever you may be right now. I also know that having accountability is great in helping us reach our goals. So if you're willing, we at *Back to the Bible* are eager to partner with you on these challenges. See Appendix 1 to see how we can make it happen together.

21

What Parents
Can Do

*Stamping out Bible illiteracy doesn't begin in the church,
the school, or the Christian college. It begins at home—your
home.*

—BARRY SHAFER

So whose job is it to teach your family the Word of God? Like
it or not, here's God's answer:

> And these words that I command you today shall be on your heart.
> You shall teach them diligently to your children, and shall talk of
> them when you sit in your house, and when you walk by the way,
> and when you lie down, and when you rise. (Deut. 6:6–7)

This Scripture passage gives parents two significant responsibilities to help their children take back the Book. First, we're to be
diligent in teaching our kids what's in the Bible and what it
means. The best way to do that is in a consistent, interesting,
daily setting that is focused around God's Word. I'm talking
about family devotions, quiet time, family altar—call it what you
want.

Second, we're to talk about what we've read in the Bible
during the normal conversation of our day. The truth of God's
Word needs to be applied to the lives of our family members.
Application is not the end of the lesson; it's an ongoing
process.

> Parents are to be the first and most important educators of their own children, diligently teaching them the Word of God. God assigned parents this non-negotiable responsibility, and children must see their Christian parents as teachers and fellow students of God's Word.
>
> —R. Albert Mohler Jr.

Parents Know Their Role but Feel Ill-Equipped

Most Christian parents I know are very aware of their responsibility to be the major spiritual and biblical influence on their children. In a recent Barna poll, nearly nine out of every ten parents of children under age thirteen (85 percent) believe they have the primary responsibility for teaching their children about biblical beliefs and spiritual matters.[1]

Teaching your children about God and his Word is clearly biblical. Paul emphatically tells us, "Fathers, do not provoke your children to anger, but bring them up in the discipline and instruction of the Lord" (Eph. 6:4). Sadly, while parents see this as a high responsibility, they admit it is not a high priority for them. So, parents, how do you fulfill this responsibility and make it a priority? Below are some suggestions.

Be Sold on Family Devotions

Having family devotions is crucial. I'm sold on family devotions. They kept my family connected as the kids were growing up. Now they are keeping my grandchildren connected to their families. Here are ten good reasons why you should have consistent family devotions in God's Word:

1) Devotions provide communication with God (Ps. 25:4–5; 119:145–52).

---

[1] "Parents Accept Responsibility for Their Child's Spiritual Development but Struggle with Effectiveness," *The Barna Update*, May 6, 2003.

2) Devotions quench our spiritual thirst (Ps. 42:1–2; 84:2; Phil. 3:10).

3) Devotions are the basis for personal spiritual growth (1 Pet. 2:2; 2 Pet. 3:18).

4) Devotions provide a safeguard against spiritual immaturity (1 Cor. 3:1–3; Ps. 119:9–11).

5) Devotions provide insight for daily living (Prov. 10:4; 17:27–28).

6) Devotions prevent schizophrenic faith (1 John 4:1; Eph. 4:11–15).

7) Devotions provide daily comfort and encouragement (Ps. 119:81; Rom. 15:4).

8) Devotions prepare us to share our faith (1 Pet. 3:15; Luke 24:27).

9) Devotions provide daily direction (Deut. 5:27; Ps. 119:105).

10) Devotions show our respect for the Bible's Author (Ps. 19:9–10; 119:127–28).

Having a family time in the Bible will not only be a link between family members, but it will also provide a safeguard against creeping Bible illiteracy in the next generation.

Family Devotionals That Work

After my wife, Linda, and I were married, we set aside a time each day to spend in God's Word together. When our children were born, they joined our family time. The first couple of years they didn't understand much, but they knew there was a special time each day when Mommy and Daddy took some time to read God's Word. Eventually the kids grew to the point they could participate in our family devotions.

Linda and I don't claim to be experts on raising children. We don't even claim to be experts on how you can have successful family devotions. But what we may lack in expertise, we make up for in experience. Our family time together worked for more than three decades and still works today. Below are some things from our experience that I trust will encourage you on how to take charge of combating Bible illiteracy in your own family.

Four Essential Components

We always made sure four essential components were a part of our family time in the Word. These aren't inspired by God; they aren't magical; they may not all be necessary. I'm simply telling you what we did that worked.

Bible Reading

The center of our devotion time was the Word of God. The purpose of our time together was to develop intimacy with God through the pages of his Word. We always read the Bible, usually a chapter a day and often read in different translations. When we finished reading, it was not uncommon for one of the kids to ask a question like, "How did your version translate the word *pavilion* in verse five?" We would then discuss the meaning of that word based on the ways different versions of the Bible would translate it. Learning was happening.

Discussion with Q&A

After we read the Word, we would spend some time discussing it to make sure we understood what it meant. This was one of my favorite elements of our devotion time because it was the most interactive. Sometimes it would stir quite a bit of laughter. Many times we'd ask questions about the things that puzzled us, or we'd ask each other questions to see if we really understood what we had just read. It was the kids' special treat to try and stump Mom and Dad. Our kids often discovered that we weren't as accomplished Bible scholars as they thought and that we were learning right with them. What an encouragement!

> **In most cases, people's spiritual beliefs are irrevocably formed when they are pre-teens.**
> —*The Barna Update,* November 17, 2003

Our question and answer time and discussions gave us the opportunity to really get to the heart of what the Bible meant. Every member of the family had equal opportunity to ask and to answer questions. We'd frequently memorize a verse or two from the passage just to tuck it away in our minds for later use.

Prayer Time

Prayer was also a key ingredient in our family devotion time. Every year we saved our Christmas cards and kept them in a basket. Each night we'd pull out a card or two and pray for the people who sent the card. That was how we formed a family prayer connection to other families. We also obtained prayer cards from some of my former students who are serving the Lord as missionaries around the world. We prayed for a missionary each night.

We prayed for our own requests too, which was always interesting. When we asked our smaller children what they wanted to pray for, their personal concerns would always surface. They would pray for school friends such as Billy because Billy's daddy wasn't living at home any more, and they didn't know why. They would pray for things important to them. Each night a different one of us would pray. I wanted my children to hear their mother and father pray as well as gain experience and skill in prayer themselves. Our prayers may have been the sweetest part of our family time.

See the World

When our children became pre-teens, I wanted them to become world Christians with a global perspective. We began first with a globe in the room. Each night we'd pray for a missionary, but only after the kids could find the country they served on the globe. Eventually I discovered Patrick Johnstone's *Operation World*,[2] so we read about a country each night and prayed specifically for it. Whoever led our family devotions read about the particular country. The rest of us

---

[2] Patrick Johnstone, *Operation World* (Grand Rapids: Zondervan, 1993).

would try to guess the capital of that country, or the literacy rate, or some other interesting fact. It became quite a competition.

Over the years my children learned about countries they never visited and peoples they will never meet. They began to see that there was a whole world out there that God loved and for whom Christ died. They saw there were other cultures and ethnic groups with needs, and the kids began to identify with those needs. It was all part of our strategy for family devotion time, and it worked.

Super Christians Not Allowed

Sometimes when I talk to people about having family devotions on a consistent basis, I get the impression that they feel too inadequate to pull it off. But we don't have to be Super Christians to influence our family. We just open the Word to them, let them learn to love it, and show them that God uses his Word to provide cohesiveness for the family. It's not easy, but it's not impossible.

One of the biggest problems you'll face is getting everyone together. Our family time wasn't long—about twenty minutes—but it occurred each day, and that's the key. We settled on a family time, immediately after dinner, and we would let nothing violate that time—nothing. If the phone rang, we didn't answer it. If the doorbell rang, we ignored it. If it was important, people would call back or come back. Our family time in God's Word was too important for interruptions, and my kids were learning that. So were their friends.

Our family devotion time together was the most important thing we did with our kids while they were growing up. As he did for us, God can use his Word to strengthen your family. God can even use his Word to heal strained relationships. He's done it for plenty of others. He can do it for you.

22

What Church Leaders Can Do

The Christians who have turned the world upside down have been men and women with a vision in their hearts and the Bible in their hands.
—T. B. MASTON

I have a very deep respect for the church and its leaders. As I mentioned in chapter 10, I began my ministry as a pastor. My father was a pastor. My older brother is a pastor. My son is a pastor. There is a plethora of pastors in my family. I respect the office of pastor. In fact, I won't let anyone call me pastor because I am now an author and Bible teacher, not a pastor.

Coupled with the youth staff and Bible study group leaders of the church, nobody has more influence in shaping the spiritual future of God's people than does the pastor. If you are the shepherd of God's flock, he has vested in you the power to lead the church "until we all attain to the unity of the faith and of the knowledge of the Son of God, to mature manhood, to the measure of the stature of the fullness of Christ" (Eph. 4:13).

The church plays a key role in reversing Bible illiteracy, but church leaders often control the degree to which the church will accomplish this unique responsibility. Without leadership little is accomplished.

It's the foot soldiers—boots on the ground—that win wars, but it's the generals who provide the leadership and guidance that make the foot soldiers successful. So what can church leaders do to call America back to the Bible? Let's investigate several types of church leaders and their roles in stamping out Bible illiteracy.

Pastors

Here's what pastors can do:

Keep the Main Thing, the Main Thing

We ask the pastors of our churches to wear a lot of hats—teacher, counselor, visitor of the sick and homebound, administrator—the list goes on. While all of these things are valuable, the importance of preaching the Word stands out above all the rest. In fact, how a pastor spends his time during the week will be reflected during his sermon on Sunday morning.

> **Preaching is the central, primary, decisive function of the church.**
>
> —Pierre Ch. Marcel

So is preaching the main thing for you? If you keep preaching as your main focus in ministry, if you spend the majority of your non-Sunday hours in preparation for being the mouthpiece for God to your people, you can be a catalyst for the recovery of Bible literacy in America, certainly in your church.

Biblical preaching is a historical distinctive of Christianity, which much of the twenty-first-century church has lost. But that doesn't have to be true in your church. Pastors have a very high privilege that not many have. They can make a difference; they can preach with passion and understanding; they can "preach the Word."

Always Give Them Something to Chew On

Over the last two decades, two important preaching journals, *Pulpit Digest* and *Preaching*, analyzed the sermons that pastors sent to them for publication. The analysis classified each sermon into one of four categories:

1) Those in which both the content of the sermon and its organization were determined by a specific biblical passage.

2) Those in which the content was explicitly biblical but the organization of the sermon was a product of the preacher's fertile mind.

3) Those in which neither the content nor the organization came from the Scripture passage but at least what the pastor said was Christian.

4) Those in which neither the content nor the organization came from a biblical passage and nothing said was obviously Christian.

Can you guess the results? In the first category there were 24.5 percent; in the second there were 22.5 percent; the third category contained 39 percent; and the fourth had 14 percent.[1]

In two decades of sermons submitted to these preaching journals, less than half were decidedly biblical in origin and organization. Less than 50 percent would have contributed in any significant way to Bible literacy in church on Sunday. But you can be different. Always give your people something to chew on. Prepare carefully. Think critically. Preach passionately. Make what you say in delivering the Word the biggest life-changer of the week for your people. Make a difference by implanting the Word of God in their hearts. Don't just talk about Bible subjects; preach the Word!

> **If the Church has lost the Word, it is not simply ill, its throat is cut.**
>
> **—John Calvin**

Centralize the Word

Ours is a techno-visual world. We love technology and must have every new gadget that hits the market. Churches are no different. Today churches use all forms of newer technologies including e-mail blasts, satellite links, video, electronic funds transfers, large-screen

---

[1] Quoted in David F. Wells, *No Place for Truth* (Grand Rapids, Eerdmans, 1993), 251–52.

projection, and more. This can be good; the church shouldn't fall behind in the understanding of technology.

But technology has had an unintended and subtle impact on Bible literacy in the church. Pastor, you can promote Bible literacy and still keep pace with technology. Traditionally, the Bible has been central to the church. But in many churches today you don't even have to bring a Bible. Anything you need to read is graphically projected onto a large screen. Most churches used to make Bibles available during services for visitors and others who did not have a Bible with them. But there has been a decline from 86 percent of churches providing pew Bibles in 2000 to 80 percent today.[2]

Now don't get me wrong—the removal of pew Bibles is not the cause of Bible illiteracy in America. To be honest, I never used a pew Bible anyway. I always brought my own Bible to church and still do. My pastor has us open our Bibles and follow along as he teaches the Word. But I believe a solid case can be made that technology, although unintended, has moved us away from the Word.

What can you do to change that? How can you centralize the Word rather than marginalize it? One quick and easy step is to read it.

Read the Word Publicly in Every Service

I remember the days when we used to read our Bibles aloud in church. We could do it then because most of us had only a King James Version and everyone read the same words at the same time (except one old guy in the back of the church). But with the large number of translations today, that has become almost impossible. Pastor, don't let that stop you! Read the Bible aloud anyway, even if you are the only one who reads. Ask your people to follow along in their Bible. As we discovered earlier, wasn't that one of the primary features of understanding the Word in Nehemiah's day?

---

[2] "Technology Use Is Growing Rapidly in Churches," *The Barna Update*, September 13, 2005.

All the people gathered as one man into the square before the Water Gate. And they told Ezra the scribe to bring the Book of the Law of Moses. . . . And he read from it . . . from early morning until midday. . . . And the ears of all the people were attentive to the Book of the Law. And Ezra the scribe stood on a wooden platform that they had made for the purpose. . . . They read from the book, from the Law of God, clearly, and they gave the sense, so that the people understood the reading. (Neh. 8:1, 3–4, 8)

The Apostle Paul told young Timothy, "Until I come, devote yourself to the public reading of Scripture, to exhortation, to teaching" (1 Tim. 4:13).

Even if everyone doesn't have the same translation, pastors can highlight the importance of the Word just by making its reading the central point in the Sunday service. The public reading of God's Word was as much a part of the church services of early Christianity as was the Lord's Table, public baptism, and worship. Make it part of your service too.

Youth Leaders

I am positive that we can reclaim Bible literacy as a society if we really want to. But in order to accomplish that, we have to reach those under twenty-one years old. We must mold and shape their life habits so they thirst for God and his Word. That's why youth pastors and leaders play such a pivotal role in the church. They are shaping the spiritual maturity of the next generation.

If you are a youth pastor or youth leader, you stand on the edge of generational change. Never underestimate your importance in the battle for Bible literacy. Here's why:

The Special Needs of Teens

According to a Gallup survey, today's teens have six basic needs that the youth leader is in an amazing position to address:

1) the need to believe that life is meaningful and has a purpose;

2) the need for a sense of community and deeper relationships;

3) the need to be appreciated and loved;

4) the need to be listened to, to be heard;

5) the need to feel that one is growing in faith;

6) the need for practical help in developing a mature faith.[3]

I don't think it's coincidental that each of these needs can be met, to some extent, by a spiritual mentor or youth ministry leader. Fully one-third of those life-needs identified by teens relate to the growth and development of faith. Teens know they need God's Word; they want to be more familiar with it, but they are not. When it comes to stamping out Bible illiteracy among teens, we are already behind. All the evidence points to the Bible knowledge among teens as being at an all-time low, and that's not good news.

Recently the Associated Press reported that the majority of American teens believe in God and worship in conventional congregations, but their religious knowledge is remarkably shallow, and they have a tough time expressing the difference that faith makes in their lives. This was according to a four-year study conducted by 133 researchers and consultants led by sociologist Christian Smith of the University of North Carolina at Chapel Hill. The results of this study can be found in the book, *Soul Searching: The Religious and Spiritual Lives of American Teenagers*.

Teens Need to Know God's Word

Gallup and Barna have also conducted surveys on teenagers. Gallup focused on Bible and religious knowledge and Barna on teens' educational experiences growing up in church and what they retained from those experiences. Gallup's research revealed that while teens believe religion is very important to them, knowing the Bible apparently isn't:

- Almost one out of ten teens believes that Moses is one of the twelve apostles.

---

[3] www.classistoronto.org/Youth/index.html.

- About one out of ten teens, when asked what Easter commemorates, responds "don't know."
- Fewer than half of teens (49 percent) knew what happened at the wedding at Cana.
- Two-thirds of teens don't know that the road to Damascus is where St. Paul was blinded by a vision of Christ.[4]

Barna's results showed that one out of every five teens (21 percent) said they did not learn anything of value during their time attending Christian churches. When asked what they learned from their exposure to the church's ministry as young children or adolescents, teens reported:

- One-quarter (26 percent) said they received general information about God, such as claims regarding his existence, his attributes, or teachings about the life of Christ.
- One-sixth (17 percent) said their church experience had imparted core religious beliefs from the Bible.
- One out of every seven (15 percent) said they learned important lifestyle principles about obeying God's laws or moral direction in life.
- Eight percent recall developing important relationships or relational skills at church.[5]

It's obvious that the special need of today's teens is not to be more religious but to be more Bible literate. When you compare the special needs of teens and what they remember about their experiences in church, a clear and special challenge is identified for all youth leaders. If you are a youth pastor or a teen leader, or have a position of influence in the lives of the teens in your church, you are in the primary position to influence and fulfill all six of the teen needs identified by the Gallup survey.

While everything that pastors can do to enhance Bible liter-

---

[4] Cited by Marie Wachlin and Bryon R. Johnson in *The Bible Literacy Report* (Fairfax, VA: The Bible Literacy Project, 2005), 6.

[5] "Teens Evaluate the Church-Based Ministry They Received As Children," *The Barna Update*, July 8, 2003.

acy in the church applies to youth pastors too, below are some additional ways for youth leaders to call America back to the Bible.

Embrace Innovation in Your Bible Study Time

Let's face it. The allure of the world is gigantic to a teen. The Internet has brought the world to their doorstep. Technology has made the games teens play something only NASA dreamed of when I was a teen. Our kids are used to being engaged, and they expect it at church too. Keeping kids involved in church, then, will require significant innovation. So embrace innovation in eternal matters. Don't let the interest or intensity decrease when fun time is over and God's time begins. That means being passionate and bold about Jesus Christ in your teaching time.

Your time in God's Word with the kids needs to be interactive, not one-dimensional. It needs to be direct—addressing issues that are not straw men but issues your teens are facing every day. And both your teaching and discussion need to come right out of the text of Scripture—not merely brush by it. The postmodern world doesn't like authority, but kids are looking for someone with answers. Be that answer person when you teach the Bible. Let God's Word be your authority, and the kids will gain an appreciation for the Bible they never had before.

Provide Positive Direction for Your Teens

Teens today need and expect direction. Youth leaders, you are in a unique position to help them understand the Bible and grow and mature into a disciple of the Lord Christ.

> Of the 51 million kids under the age of 18 who live in the United States, more than 40 million of them do not know Jesus Christ as their Savior.
>
> —*The Barna Update,* May 6, 2003

What you do with your kids ought to be fun and innovative. But it also has to have direction and purpose. Avoid the temptation to make your time with your teens little more than "stupid pet tricks."[6] Make the most of your opportunity to help teens capture the Bible at the prime time in their lives. Present a genuine forum for their spiritual growth. Prepare them for life.

When you finish instructing your teens, ask them what difference your time together has had on their destiny. Push them to think in terms of the eternal and to respond to you in those terms. You can be sure they'll be honest. If no one can identify the eternal in your time together it's probably because you didn't go anywhere. Always make sure you have a spiritual target with your kids, and if you don't hit it, go back and rethink your strategy.

Meeting a Third of Teens' Basic Needs

Today's teens have very special needs. They need to know that adults love them and believe in them. If you're a youth pastor or youth leader you know how tough it is to be a teenager in today's world. They are in the most formative years of their lives. This is the perfect time to establish life habits, and your influence as a youth leader is a primary factor in establishing those habits. So make sure the habit of Bible discovery is a big part of that influence. Help them spend the rest of their lives benefiting from their love for God's Word.

---

[6] At a New Year's Eve lock-in at a church in Indiana, a youth leader munched on a mixture of dog food, sardines, potted meat, sauerkraut, cottage cheese, and salsa, topped off with holiday eggnog. The kids were grossed out and loved it. Then he spit out the gastric mixture into a glass and encouraged youth group members to drink it! Four sets of parents are suing the church (no joke). According to an *Associated Press* account, the youth pastor said that the "gross-out" game, called the *Human Vegematic*, was just for fun. No one was forced to participate. Says Gene Edward Veith, "Such 'gross-out' games have become a fad in youth ministry. Since adolescents are amused by bodily functions, crude behavior, and tastelessness—following the church-growth principle of giving people what they like as a way to entice them into the kingdom—many evangelical youth leaders think this is a way to reach young people. What do teenagers learn from these youth group activities? Nothing of the Bible. Nothing of theology. Nothing of the cost of discipleship. . . . Teenagers get enough entertainment, psychology, and hedonism from their culture. They don't need it from their church. What they need—and often yearn for—is God's Word and spiritual formation." Gene Edward Veith, "Stupid Church Tricks." *World Magazine*, August 24, 2002.

Sunday School Teachers and
Bible Study Leaders

Sunday school was begun in Gloucester, England, in 1780 by Robert Raikes. His goal was to get the kids off the street and help them read and understand the Bible. By 1831, Sunday school in Great Britain was ministering weekly to 1,250,000 children, approximately 25 percent of the population.[7]

While Sunday school continues strong in the United States, small-group Bible studies have replaced the traditional standardized Sunday school program in many churches.[8]

Regardless of whether your church uses the Sunday school, the small-group model, or both, the bottom line must always be the study of God's Word. Fellowship is important. Networking is huge in the twenty-first century. But in order to take back the Book, our "growth groups" and Sunday school classes must be all about the Book. You as the leader can make the difference. You have a privileged position in calling America back to the Bible. Don't take it lightly.

---

[7] *Wikipedia*, "Sunday School."

[8] "Sunday School Is Changing in Under-the-Radar but Significant Ways," *The Barna Update*, July 11, 2005.

23

What Churches
Can Do

As we esteem the gift of teaching and those who teach well, we will help bring about the rebirth of biblical literacy and informed faith in North America.

—GARY BURGE

A major player in the recovery of Bible literacy in America is the local church. If the church is blind to the extent of its Bible illiteracy, if the church cannot honestly detect the cancer eating away at its foundation, then the foundation will be destroyed (Ps. 11:3).

Churches are composed of Christ-followers (or at least they should be). They are people who have been saved by grace, live by faith, and love those who have not yet found the Savior. The church is the staging ground for moving out into the world with the Good News. But it is also the training center where soldiers are equipped for hand-to-hand combat with Satan. It's this equipping role where churches need to step up today.

No Lone Rangers

While faith in Christ is a private matter and must be expressed personally to enjoy God's salvation, the expression of that faith has always had a corporate dimension to it. In Old Testament Israel there were no Jews: there were Israelites. The Apostle Paul described the church as a body with each of its parts interdependent and interrelated (1 Cor. 12:12–27). There are vital aspects of our Christian experience that simply cannot be successful alone, disconnected from the people of God. If community is the way to grow and mature the church, then the local church must be the center of Bible education for its members.

The church has unique responsibility and opportunity in the recovery of Bible literacy. It is in the context of the local church that Paul challenged specially gifted servants "to equip the saints for the work of ministry, for building up the body of Christ" (Eph. 4:12).

> A crisis of basic biblical and theological literacy exists in America's churches, and church leaders must do all they can to address this growing problem.
> —Michael J. Vlach

Churches Must Do Some Gut-Wrenching Self-Appraisal

When I was growing up, the church was often (and rightly so) accused of being self-absorbed. If an unsaved person wandered into the church service, you could be certain it was entirely by accident. Then along came the seeker movement and changed all that. But with the seeker movement came some unexpected, and, I trust, unwanted consequences.

Today, churches are filled with many unbelievers who are not active, growing members of the body of Christ. This impacts Bible illiteracy in the church. A recent Barna study reported that "only 41 percent of adults in America's twelve largest denominations could be classified as 'born again.'"[1]

For the past four years, The Gallup Organization has surveyed members of United States religious communities to determine their level of engagement with their congregations and their individual level of spiritual commitment. Surprisingly, only 19 percent of congregation members were fully spiritually committed in 2002, with that number increasing to 22 percent in 2004.[2]

---

[1] For more information about the makeup of the evangelical church, see "The State of the Church, 2000," *The Barna Update*, March 21, 2000.
[2] Albert L. Winseman, "Does Congregation Membership Imply Spiritual Commitment? *Gallup Poll News Survey*, August 9, 2005.

Oddly, pastors seem to be less in tune with the degree of Bible illiteracy and spiritual immaturity in their church than their members are. Based on interviews with a representative national sample of 627 Protestant pastors, The Barna Group discovered that pastors believe the majority of their people are deeply committed to God and well along the road to spiritual maturity. In fact, as many as one out of every six pastors (16 percent) believes that 90 percent or more of the adults in their church hold their relationship with God as their top priority in life.[3]

In contrast, a national survey of 1,002 adults asked the same question—identify their top priority in life—and only one out of every seven adults (15 percent) placed their faith in God at the top of their priority list. When the survey isolated those who attend Protestant churches, not quite one out of every four (23 percent) named their faith in God as their top priority in life.[4] Pastors sometimes see their people through rose-colored glasses. Bible illiteracy runs much deeper in the church than most pastors think.

Churches Must Assess the Bible Knowledge of Their People

Perhaps the greatest hindrance to knowledge is a failure to know what you don't know. I fear this is true in the evangelical church. We don't have a clue how little we know about the Bible.

So how do we assess our Bible knowledge? At this point I have more questions than answers. But when I talk about the church assessing the Bible knowledge of its people, I'm not proposing a threatening, fill-in-the-blank, pencils-down, close-your-test-booklet nightmare. Nor am I suggesting a church version of *Jeopardy!* or Trivial Pursuit. I am proposing some sort of periodic, quantifiable method of assessing a Christian's knowledge and understanding of

---

[3] "Surveys Show Pastors Claim Congregants Are Deeply Committed to God but Congregants Deny It!" *The Barna Update*, January 20, 2006.
[4] Ibid.

the Word so that both the church and the individual can chart their spiritual growth.

Before you shudder at that possibility, think of the fact that the church quantifies everything. We know the exact square footage of our church plant building. We can talk about how many people attended our services because ushers count them. The church financial officer knows exactly how much was received in each offering because people count it. We know how many people our auditorium seats, how many acres of land we own, and how much money we have to increase the budget for next year.

If we are not opposed to measuring all those temporal things, why are we so loathe to measure that which truly counts in church growth—the growth toward spiritual maturity of our people? Why do we make no effort to chart spiritual growth when we go to such lengths to chart numerical growth? Anyone brave enough to answer?

Testing Core Knowledge

Any Bible literacy test given should include an assessment of core knowledge (information we know), core competencies (our ability to understand, interpret, and then apply Scripture), and core behavior (changed behavior as a result of reading and understanding the Bible). These three things ought to be examined for every Christ-follower at various stages of our spiritual journey.

Who will determine the various stages of core Bible knowledge? Each local church will. Get your pastoral staff and some key lay leaders together some Saturday, brew some coffee, and start talking about it. Look at examples that other pastors have used for their congregations as a starting point. I've seen one that adult ministries pastor Jim Levitt of Bethel Evangelical Free Church in Fargo, North Dakota, devised for his people. It was a spiritual maturity index that wasn't about Bible trivia; it was about spiritual competencies based on Bible knowledge. You could do the same with a little thought and effort. Until you know what you do or do not know, you can't map out a strategy for the journey to full spiritual maturity.

Testing Core Competencies

The first step toward Bible literacy is always Bible reading. But while reading is fundamental, it isn't an end in itself. Being Bible literate also requires that we possess core competencies—that is, knowing and understanding Bible facts, being able to interpret them, and then applying them to the way we live. Thus, any test for Bible literacy must include core competencies.

> Bible literacy should be a key measuring stick for every Sunday school. If it isn't, you're putting your kids' faith and future of the Church at risk.
>
> —Neil MacQueen

What are some specific core competencies a church should be concerned about for its people? You'll determine which ones are important for your church, but to be biblically literate, I think a person should know how to take a passage of Scripture and be able to do the following:

- relate it to the context of the Scripture around it;
- explain the primary intent of the writer based on the context;
- pair the truth of this passage with other biblical passages;
- apply the primary truth of the passage to your life situation;
- use the passage of Scripture to defend what you believe.

Testing Core Behavior

Core behavior is also a part of being Bible literate. Testing core behavior is simply determining what changes in behavior have occurred as a result of reading and interpreting the Bible. It's asking the question, "How will I live differently because I have encountered God in his Word?" Again, you will determine what behavioral changes prayerfully need to take place in your church as a result of growing Bible literacy, but here are a few that I would suggest:

- a deepening thirst for God that causes you to return to his

Word, prompted not by guilt but by sheer longing to know him better (Ps. 42:1–2);

- a boldness in lifestyle that is evident to all you encounter because they have taken note that you have been with Jesus (Acts 4:13);
- a demonstrable joy that permeates your life because of the inner strength you have received through the Word by the Holy Spirit (Neh. 8:10);
- a desire to live in holiness because you want to be like God and want him to be pleased with you (1 Pet. 1:15–16).

The church must play the major role in the recovery of Bible literacy because, along with the family and the individual, the church bears much of the responsibility for the core knowledge, core competencies, and core behavior of those who are obedient to God. If the church doesn't step up, no one will follow.

24

What Others Are Doing

Make no little plans. They have no magic to stir men's blood. Make big plans: aim high in hope and work.

—DANIEL HUDSON BURNHAM

If the Bible were returned to every classroom in America and studied as a textbook, it would benefit our country, but it wouldn't stamp out Bible illiteracy. If a Bible were placed in every hotel room, at every restaurant table, and in every hand in America, that in itself wouldn't cause the restoration of Bible literacy. Owning a Bible isn't the same as reading it and living by what it says. Bible illiteracy didn't overwhelm our nation overnight and it won't be wiped out overnight.

Here's the good news: some are taking the problem seriously. There is growing discussion, increasing numbers of magazine articles, and more Christian leaders who at least acknowledge that Bible illiteracy is eating the twenty-first-century church alive. In this chapter, we want to focus on some heads that are sticking up.

Prairie Dogs

You've probably seen pictures of them or visited one of their "towns." They are prairie dogs, robust rodents related to ground squirrels, chipmunks, and marmots. Prairie dogs are of the genus *Cynomys* (Greek for *mouse dog*). The early pioneers and settlers passing through the heartland of the United States called them *dogs* or *sod poodles* because of their high-pitched, bark-like call.

Tourists enjoy prairie dogs because they stick their heads up out of their burrowed holes and "bark." Actually, when a predator approaches, the first alert prairie dog gives sharp, two-syllable warning barks (about forty per minute), bobs up and down in excitement, and then disappears back in his hole. It's when you see heads sticking up that you know prairie dogs have taken notice of a predator and are preparing for action. Today, in the Christian community, heads are sticking up.

> After plummeting to a twenty-year low of just 31 percent in 1995, Bible readership rose to 47 percent of adults during a typical week in 2006.
> —*The Barna Update,* April 3, 2006

Like the prairie dogs of the Great Plains, I see evidence of alertness to the plague of Bible illiteracy that I haven't seen in a quarter of a century. I believe something is about to happen in America to address this problem. I also believe that you and I will be a part of the solution.

Preachers

A growing number of pastors are expressing frustration at the lack of understanding of God's Word among their people. For months I've been traveling the United States seeking to build a Bible alliance of pastors, professors, and just ordinary people concerned about Bible illiteracy in America. I have encountered some pastors who just don't see a problem. They are like the proverbial ostrich. But others see the problem clearly and are beginning to sound the alarm. They are like the prairie dog.

One of the great churches of our time is Tenth Presbyterian Church of Philadelphia, part of the Presbyterian Church in America (PCA) denomination.[1] Affectionately known as "Tenth" or "Tenth Pres," this church has had an incredible history of faithfulness in

---

[1] www.tenth.org.

teaching the Word of God. When one thinks of Tenth, one automatically thinks of Donald Grey Barnhouse or James Montgomery Boice, and stepping up nicely to fill the shoes of his predecessors is current senior minister, Philip G. Ryken. The tradition of strong Bible exposition at Tenth continues.

Chuck Smith, pastor of Calvary Chapel[2] in Costa Mesa, California, has had a profound impact on expository preaching in the Calvary Chapel movement. Churches in those associated fellowships have always exhibited a strong commitment to the exposition of the Word. Recently I sat down with Bob Botsford, senior pastor of Horizon North County Christian Fellowship[3] in Rancho Santa Fe, California. His passion for preaching God's Word expositionally was a breath of fresh air to me. Mike MacIntosh has been pastor of Horizon Christian Fellowship[4] in San Diego, California, for more than thirty years. In his book, *Falling in Love with the Bible*,[5] Mike challenges us to change our mind-set for reading God's Word from obligation to delight. We need that.

Southern Baptist pastors have always been energetic evangelists, but more and more within the Southern Baptist Convention (SBC) pastors are seeing the need for solid Bible teaching. The gargantuan Prestonwood Baptist Church[6] in Plano, Texas, is a good example. In a recent meeting with pastor Jack Graham and teaching pastor David McKinley, I found not only a warm reception to helping in the battle for Bible literacy but a ready environment in which to test what teenagers know of God's Word and how we can creatively reach them with more truth from the Word.

Fighting Bible illiteracy has always been a cornerstone of John MacArthur's ministry at Grace Community Church[7] in Sun Valley, California. Out of a strong pulpit ministry has come a variety of associated ministries, such as The Master's College, The Master's

---

[2] www.calvarychapel.org.
[3] www.horizon.org.
[4] www.horizonsd.org.
[5] Mike MacIntosh, *Falling in Love with the Bible* (Colorado Springs, CO: Cook, 2005).
[6] www.prestonwood.org.
[7] www.gracechurch.org.

Seminary, *Grace to You* radio, and The Master's Academy, which trains indigenous church leaders. Through his preaching, writing, and shepherding ministries, John MacArthur has been a warrior in the battle for Bible literacy.

> No one in the English speaking world can be considered literate without a basic knowledge of the Bible.
> —*The New Dictionary of Cultural Literacy*

There are many others, of course, too numerous to mention. But here's the real kicker. The genuine heroes of Bible exposition don't tend to be the big names of radio and television or even the big churches. They are the pastors faithful to the Word in small and medium-sized churches everywhere. Be encouraged. I am—much more so than I was a decade ago. Maybe the church is finally getting the message. Maybe we're ready to begin strategizing to call America back to the Bible.

Para-Church Ministries Working for Bible Literacy

I am hesitant to name names because very important ministries in the fight against Bible illiteracy will be left out. But you should know that those dedicated to stamping out Bible illiteracy are not phantoms. They are real ministries, dedicated and worthy of your investigation. Each of them is addressing the problem of Bible illiteracy in some way.

The American Bible Society

Founded in 1816 in New York City, the American Bible Society continues to be a leader and an innovator in providing resources both for translation and distribution of the Bible as well as individual help in reading and understanding the Bible. Recently I met with their leadership team at their headquarters on Broadway and discovered hearts that beat for Bible literacy. I was encouraged. They are doing significant things.[8]

The National Bible Association

Located in the heart of New York City, the National Bible Association was created in 1940 by a group of business and professional people. The signature event for the National Bible Association is their sponsorship of the National Bible Week. The very first National Bible Week was planned for December 8–14, 1941, but it was interrupted by the attack on Pearl Harbor. However, National Bible Week has been celebrated each year since.[9]

Scripture Union

Scripture Union (located in Milton Keynes, England) seeks to use the Bible to inspire children, young people, and adults around the world to know God. They are currently in research and development of a Scripture Engagement Operating System (SEOS) which will allow people to better understand the Bible and build a habit of daily Bible reading.[10]

Neighborhood Bible Studies

Neighborhood Bible Studies is a not-for-profit ministry begun in 1960. It is primarily committed to evangelism through small group discussion Bible studies. Through inductive Bible study, men and women have the opportunity to make informed decisions in response to the claims of Scripture on their lives and to mature in Christian faith. Their headquarters is in Dobbs Ferry, New York.[11]

---

[8] www.americanbible.org.
[9] www.nationalbible.org.
[10] www.scriptureunion.org.uk.
[11] www.neighborhoodbiblestudy.org.

Bible Study Fellowship

Bible Study Fellowship International (BSF) is a San Antonio, Texas-based, interdenominational, lay-Christian organization with Bible study classes in cities across the United States and around the world. BSF offers day classes for women, as well as evening classes for men, women, and single young adults (ages 18–35).[12]

Precept Ministries

In the late 1960s, Jack Arthur was station manager for a Christian radio station in Chattanooga, Tennessee. His wife, Kay, started teaching a teen Bible class in their living room. By 1970 the class was so large, it began meeting in a barn. Today the teaching ministry of Kay Arthur, primarily to women, extends around the world in over one hundred countries. Both Jack and Kay are passionate about Bible literacy and dedicated to winning the battle.[13]

Living Proof Ministries

The mission statement of Living Proof Ministries (LPM) indicates that the organization is dedicated to "Biblical literacy and a commitment to guide believers to love and live on God's Word." This is accomplished primarily through the writing, speaking, and teaching of Houston-based Beth Moore. Beth's audience is diverse, but it is young women who seem to benefit most from her teaching through Living Proof Ministries.[14]

InWord Ministries

Founded in 1996 in response to widespread biblical illiteracy among teens, InWord is a Middletown, Ohio-based, non-denominational, non-profit Bible ministry seeking to fill the vacuum of resources devoted to equipping teens with the Word of God. Barry Shafer,

---

[12] www.bsfinternational.org.
[13] www.precept.org.
[14] www.lproof.org.

InWord founder, served as a full-time church youth pastor where he developed both a personal passion for knowing God through his Word and a desire to help teenagers, young adults, and other youth workers become equipped with an accurate understanding of the Bible.[15]

> The percent of adults in California, Oregon, and Washington that read the Bible has risen from 29 percent in 1994 to 44 percent in 2004.
>
> —*The Barna Update,* March 1, 2004

Walk Thru the Bible

Walk Thru the Bible (WTTB) has hosted more than two million participants in its live Bible seminars since 1976. The WTTB approach is unique, fun, interactive, and instructive. The organization walks participants through the Bible without note taking or lectures. Instead, they see learning the Bible as a creative and interactive adventure. Approximately three out of four people who attend the Atlanta-based Walk Thru the Bible seminars commit to read the Bible and pray every day.[16]

Child Evangelism Fellowship

For almost seventy years Child Evangelism Fellowship (CEF) has been used of God to evangelize boys and girls with the gospel of Jesus Christ and to disciple them in the Word of God. With workers in more than 150 countries around the world, CEF is passionate about bringing children into a right relationship with God and then teaching them in God's Word to help them mature in their faith. One of CEF's primary goals is to see boys and girls established in Bible-teaching churches.

---

[15] www.inword.org.
[16] www.walkthru.org.

Many More

There are many others, of course—Bible societies, Bible-teaching ministries, media and film ministries—but if you're a Christian looking for help with your own battle for Bible literacy, rest assured, help is out there.

You should be encouraged that after the long drought of hearing God's Word, heads are sticking up. People are doing something about Bible illiteracy. It's like Elijah's servant seeing a little cloud the size of a man's hand rising from the sea after a long drought (1 Kings 18:44), God is awakening the sleeping giant of the church to its number-one threat, and for that you and I can be encouraged and praise the Lord.

25

What The Bible Literacy Center Is Doing

When I first arrived at Yale, even those who came from nonreligious backgrounds knew the Bible better than most of those now who come from churchgoing families.

—GEORGE LINDBECK

In response to the national crisis of Bible illiteracy, the international media ministry *Back to the Bible* established The Bible Literacy Center (BLC)[1] in March 2006. The Bible Literacy Center is a research and development organization seeking to provide data about why people do or do not read their Bible and then identify practical ways to connect people personally with God's Word.

The mission is very focused on answering one question: "Why do so many people own Bibles but so few read them?" This is the most widespread problem in the Christian church today, and in order to solve this problem it must first clearly be defined and examined. Anecdotes will not do; hard data is needed. The Bible Literacy Center is gathering the hard data necessary—first, to understand the problem and second, to develop solutions to the problem. Once core reasons for Bible illiteracy are identified, a variety of strategies are formulated and appropriate tools developed that will help solve the problem.

> More than 90 percent of people surveyed spend less than one hour a week reading the Bible.
>
> —The Bible Literacy Center, May 18, 2006

---

[1] Contact The Bible Literacy Center at bibleliteracycenter.com or at P.O. Box 82808, Lincoln, NE 68501.

The Bible Literacy Center is unique in addressing Bible illiteracy in its ongoing commitment to solving this problem through a multi-phase, cross-functional approach. At the BLC facilities in Lincoln, Nebraska, a state-of-the-art research facility has been created that allows onsite surveys, web-based surveys, interviews, behavioral analysis, and other research methods. The Center is also equipped for conducting research offsite at locations such as churches, camps, conventions, and crusades across the nation. The last survey done by the BLC questioned 8,600 participants.

The Bible Literacy Center consists of three main components: the Research Technology Center, the Product Development Center, and the Connection Center.

The Research Technology Center

The Research Technology Center is where the question "Why do so many people own Bibles but so few read them?" is examined. Data is gathered through a multi-phase, multi-level research study using a variety of research tools, including extensive written surveys, interviews, Internet-based surveys for specific audiences, behavioral analysis, focus groups, and other proven research methods.

The research process targets different age groups and demographic audiences. By instituting research around age and life experiences, each audience is examined both individually and in comparison with others. The BLC researchers look for common identifiers as well as distinctions that could be unique to an age group or a target audience. For example, the way in which a teenager views life could impact his or her thinking about the absolute standards found in Scripture. The teen's views and rationale could be considerably different from that of the teen's parents or grandparents.

Although The Bible Literacy Center is researching all age groups, special emphasis is being put on research targeted at understanding the thinking of younger people, ages eight to twenty-one. That's because this age group is the most biblically illiterate, yet they will direct the future of this nation.

Six out of ten teens believe that a good person can earn
eternal salvation through good deeds.
—*The Barna Update,* October 23, 2000

While the Bible remains a respected text among most young adults
(three out of five teens say they believe the Bible is totally accurate
in all that it teaches), many teens embrace views today that are anything but biblical. For instance, two-thirds think that Satan is not a
living being but merely a symbol of evil.[2]

Dr. Arnie Cole, chief research officer of The Bible Literacy
Center, says, "If these teens are the future of the church, we
absolutely must find a way to get them into the Word in a meaningful way. We don't want to load them up with facts or trivia; we
want them to encounter God when they read his Word. That will
take behavioral change and we are interested in nothing less. We
have to develop behavior patterns that keep this generation from
falling into the snare of Bible illiteracy as previous generations have
done."[3] It is absolutely critical that we find ways to help teenagers
personally connect with God and discover the Bible as a valuable
source of guidance for daily living.

The Product Development Center

The Product Development Center utilizes the research findings of the
Research Technology Center to formulate new tools that will help all
age groups, especially youth, connect personally with the Bible.
These products are then field tested in controlled venues where direct
feedback can be obtained and usage can be monitored. Venues such
as our own Connection Center, or Edge64, are used to test the products and ensure they are meeting their intended objectives. Field testing is also done in order to guard against demographic or geographic
anomalies. Based on feedback from the teen and other users, the

---

[2] "Teenagers' Beliefs Moving Farther from Biblical Perspectives," *The Barna Update,* October 23, 2000.
[3] Arnold Cole, The Bible Literacy Center.

product will either be placed in mass production and distribution or be sent back to the Research Technology and Product Development Centers for further research and revisions.

The BLC is a cooperating member of the National Network of Youth Ministries. This is a twenty-five-year-old network of major denominations and parachurch ministries that focus on the spiritual needs of America's youth. The Network's "Cooperating Ministries" are a partnership of national ministries who agree to network their efforts to reach and disciple every teenager for Christ. Through partnerships, these ministries share resources, programs, and expertise across organizational lines to accomplish a common vision. In order to increase effectiveness in areas of special need, "Affinity Networks" are formed (such as Campus Alliance representing over seventy ministries—rural, urban, Native American, and missions) to accomplish together what could never be accomplished alone.

Through partnership with the National Network of Youth Ministries, the BLC and particularly the Product Development Center create unique resources that will draw teens and pre-teens into a lifelong and meaningful relationship with Scripture.

The Connection Center

The Connection Center, also known as Edge64, is based at the *Back to the Bible* International headquarters in Lincoln, Nebraska. It has the look and feel of a café, a music and concert venue, and an indoor skate park. It is all of these, but more importantly, it's also a working laboratory where concepts are tested in a real-life environment. Professional observers use surveys and observation as a springboard both to test the data received from the Research Technology Center and to test the resources developed by the Product Development Center.

The research results have provided important insights and findings to thousands of church and ministry leaders who recognize there is a serious problem and who share a concern about the Bible illiteracy crisis impacting every aspect of this nation. The intent of this research is to empower Christian ministries to formulate meaningful action plans to turn this tide of illiteracy by using and applying the research findings. The Bible Literacy Center has developed new products and tools based on research findings that will help individuals of all ages connect with the truths of God's Word.

> **53 percent of teens believe Jesus committed sins while He was on earth. Even more troublesome, this is the view of 40 percent of born again teens and 52 percent of all teens who attend a Protestant church.**
> —*The Barna Update,* October 8, 2002

The Edge64 café is a perfect environment for middle school, high school, college, and university students to entertain ideas taken from the Bible and for testing how this demographic group best relates to God and his Word. Here they find a place of acceptance and substance—acceptance for who they are, substance from the Bible for who they will become.[4]

Skate the Edge, a fully equipped indoor skate park, attracts teens and pre-teens by the hundreds. They skate a while and then sit out a while. While they are between skating sessions, trained BLC staff engage them in discussion about the Bible, its importance, and their understanding of it. For those interested, Bible study groups are formed and the *down time* from skateboarding becomes the *up time* for mentoring.

It Takes a Movement

The Bible Literacy Center's research team is aware that the challenge of overcoming Bible illiteracy is far greater than any one min-

---

[4] "In a nutshell, Mosaics are looking for an authentic experience with God and other people," explained George Barna. "Teenagers patronize churches and other event-oriented organizations because they are seeking a compelling experience that is made complete and safe by the presence of people they know and trust, and from whom they are willing to learn and take their cues. Music and other ambient factors may attract them once or twice, but those elements will not keep them coming back for more. There has to be sufficient substance, quality, hope, and genuine mutual concern and acceptance for them to return." "Teens Change Their Tune Regarding Self and Church," *The Barna Update*, April 23, 2002.

istry can address. That's why the BLC seeks to work in collaboration with other ministries who share the Center's concern for the lack of Bible literacy in America.

Ultimately, the prayer of The Bible Literacy Center is that God will begin a movement, a movement that will require a cooperative alliance of leaders and ministries who have the same concern for people, young and old, and are willing to work together to call America back to the Bible.

Conclusion:
It's Time to Attack

*My center is giving way, my right is retreating. Situation excellent.
I shall attack.*

—FIELD MARSHALL FERDINAND FOCH

Field Marshall Ferdinand Foch was the World War I supreme commander of the Allied forces in France. He turned the tide of war when he halted the German advance during the second battle of Marne in July 1918. Several months later he accepted the Germans' surrender. One of my favorite quotes is the one from the field marshall quoted at the beginning of this chapter. It seems so appropriate in the battle for Bible literacy.

With Americans at an all-time low in Bible knowledge, and with no noticeable difference between the Bible knowledge of those in church and those outside, this is definitely the time to attack. Our center has already given way and our right is retreating. But there is good reason to be optimistic, even though much of what you have read in this book may have given you spiritual heartburn.

Having now wrestled with the plague of Bible illiteracy in America for more than a quarter of a century, I have come to some conclusions. These conclusions are based on hard research, credible experience, and biblical truth. I want to share them with you.

The Real Problem

The real problem in the face of this epidemic of Bible illiteracy is that most people, including most Christians, are not ready to accept the responsibility for their ignorance of the only Book God ever wrote. Accepting responsibility has never been easy. It's even more difficult now for three reasons.

The Secularization of American Society

Old America was religious in lifestyle and attitudes; New America is secular in lifestyle and attitudes. The secularization of American society has diminished the role of the Bible in advising—even governing—the way we live. As a result, people read the Bible less because they see less value in what it says. Thus, the average American accepts no responsibility to live biblically as our forefathers did because, by and large, we don't even know what living biblically means in the twenty-first century.

The Death of Stigma

Another significant deterrent to accepting personal responsibility for not reading the Bible is the death of stigma. A *New York Times* article reported that the out-of-wedlock birthrate in Harlem was 89 percent. But what was most remarkable about the article, especially considering its source, was that it gave as one of the reasons for this high illegitimacy rate the lack of stigma over being a single mother. Remove stigma and the problem goes away.[1]

When there was societal stigma at being biblically ignorant, people read their Bibles to avoid that stigma. But today there is no stigma attached to biblical ignorance, so fewer people feel compelled to take the personal responsibility to read, to know, or to obey what God has said.

> **What we must do is to educate the masses of the people up to the Bible, not bring the Bible down to their level.**
> —Martyn Lloyd-Jones

Accountability Only to Yourself

With the dawn of secularism as the religion of "new" America, and without the stigma of being ignorant of God and his Word, postmodernism overtook America, and everyone became their

---

[1] Dennis Prager, "The American Tradition of Personal Responsibility," *Heritage Lecture 515*, September 20, 1994, www.heritage.org/Research/PoliticalPhilosophy/HL515.cfm.

own standard for right or wrong. Americans became account-able only to themselves, picking and choosing what they deemed as good or bad for them. How they feel trumps what they know. We have no accountability to anyone or anything but our own feelings.

Failure to accept personal responsibility is a strong deterrent for Americans—including most evangelicals—to reading God's Word and being fulfilled as a result. We know we should; we don't care if we fail.

The Real Need

The real key to calling America back to the Bible isn't more money, more products, more plans, or more programs. We have more than enough study Bibles, reading guides, books, and DVDs, and a plethora of other resources to win the war on Bible illiteracy—if any of these were the key to victory. The fact is they aren't. The real need is behavioral. We need to change our behavior if we are to win this war.

The Behavior of Coordinated Effort

One necessary behavioral change is the American penchant for indi-vidualism. Lone Rangers and Don Quixotes don't defeat Satan; troops who have locked arms do.

Winning this battle will take a coordinated effort by pastors, churches, educators, parents, and all of us locking arms and fight-ing on multiple battlefronts simultaneously. We need each other. That's why the United States military has multiple branches; there are multiple tasks and talents necessary to win a war. Let's not be sat-isfied with shooting at Satan with our rifle when we could lock arms and fire a canon.

The Behavior of Priorities

It's time we stop tiptoeing around the real need in the battle for Bible literacy. The real behavioral need for Christians is to stop whining and get real. Let's be honest enough to admit that the reason we fail in reading God's Word is not because we don't have time or the Bible is too hard to understand. We don't read the Bible because we haven't made it a habit in our lives.

God will not be shoehorned into our day. He won't be *Plan B*. He won't wait in the wings for us to fit him into our busy schedule. But if we decide to change our behavior, God will make sure we get done everything we need to in our day.

The Behavior of Discipline

You knew I'd get to this. I've been putting it off. We don't read our Bible because we lack the discipline. I have had good, hearty Christians tell me they haven't read Leviticus or the Song of Solomon or Ezekiel ever! These are not spiritual sissies; these are pastors' wives, Sunday school teachers, Bible study leaders. And why? They tried it once and found it too hard.

> **Most Christians are not disciplined enough to sustain study. Because discipline is hard work, many believers choose to let others draw biblical conclusions for them.**
> —Judy Lunsford

Let's apply that same logic to other areas of life. When the boss asks you why you haven't been selling to a certain lucrative demographic, do you respond, *I tried it once and it was too hard*? Does the HIV/AIDS researcher give up on a promising procedure because, *I tried it once and it was too hard*? Our excuses sound a bit ridiculous when applied to other areas of our lives.

The key to winning the battle for Bible literacy is behavior change, not new products, new programs, or new Bibles. Americans don't need more Bibles; we need to read the ones we have. That will require behavioral change.

The Real Hope

The future is as bright as the promises of God, and God promised, "So shall my word be that goes out from my mouth; it shall not return to me empty, but it shall accomplish that which I purpose, and shall succeed in the thing for which I sent it" (Isa. 55:11). So what is the real hope in winning the battle for Bible literacy? Maybe it's not what you think.

Developed Behavior, Not Changed Behavior

The hope for the future of Bible literacy comes from developing behavior, not changing it. After people have lived a certain way for a long period of time, changing their behavior is almost impossible. Developed behavior is far more probable.

Suppose The Bible Literacy Center discovers the disconnect between people owning a Bible and reading it. What will they do with that information?

They could tell my generation that we have to change our behavior. Good luck with that! My generation has already lived most of its life; we're too set in our ways. Changing behavior is not the answer.

Developed Behavior in the Young

The answer is to get to that demographic group in which behavioral patterns are still developing. We need to discover what will connect young people with God's Word and work on helping them develop a lifestyle that doesn't leave God and his Word in life's wings.

> I think a new world will arise out of the religious mists when we approach the Bible with the idea that it is not only a book which was once spoken, but a book which is now speaking.
>
> —A. W. Tozer

The key to Bible literacy in America is to develop the behavior of Mosaics, not just to try to change the behavior of Baby Boomers and

Seniors.[2] That may not be comforting to you, but this is the age group that is forming life patterns and belief systems. We dare not forfeit this generation to their peers, to secularists, or to Satan, or we will lose the battle.

Developed Behavior for Life

Sitting in the office of pollster George Barna one day, I told him of my plans to attack the problem of Bible illiteracy in the fifteen- to twenty-year-old demographic (I only use these terms around pollsters). He looked me in the eye and said, "You're too late. Our research tells us that if a person trusts Christ as Savior during childhood, by age eight they will have learned essentially everything they will ever know about the Bible." I was shocked. I hope he's wrong. He probably isn't.

This is important for all you parents, pastors, teachers, youth leaders—anyone who has any influence on teens and pre-teens. If you can get to them at their current age and convince them they're robbing themselves by not reading and living by God's Word, you'll form attitudes and behaviors that will last a lifetime.

It's Time to Attack

It's time we sent a message to the old snake that we will not go quietly into the night. We will not retreat. We will not surrender. We will attack. Bible illiteracy can be stamped out in America. In fact, if you take action now to see that you win your personal battle for Bible literacy, and those in your church win their battle, and I win my battle, we'll begin to put the shakes in the devil. Satan fears no person more than a biblically literate Christian. We are his greatest human threat on the battlefield.

So, let's attack the plague of Bible illiteracy with vigor and in the power of God's Holy Spirit. Don't allow all the statistical bad

---

[2] Age group designations used throughout this book are: Mosaics—those born 1984–2002; Busters—those born 1965–1983; Boomers—those born 1946–1964; Elders or Seniors—those born before 1945.

news to scare you. Yes, the problem of Bible illiteracy in America is epidemic in proportion, but don't ever forget: "He who is in you is greater than he who is in the world" (1 John 4:4). We need to know the bad news before we can appreciate the good news, and there is good news. Once we admit how bad things are, let's allow the Lord Christ to show us how good they can become. Let's attack.

Go back and review all the things that can be done to call America back to the Bible. Read again what churches can do, and parents can do, and you can do. Then, as the television commercial says, "Just do it."

And let's not just concentrate on ourselves. Let's fight and not declare victory until every teen and pre-teen in America says, "How sweet are your words to my taste, sweeter than honey to my mouth! Through your precepts I get understanding; therefore I hate every false way. Your word is a lamp to my feet and a light to my path. I have sworn an oath and confirmed it, to keep your righteous rules" (Ps. 119:103–106).

That's when we can again sing with honesty, "America! America! God shed his grace on thee."[3]

---

[3] Katharine Lee Bates, *America the Beautiful*. Falmouth Historical Society.

Appendix
One

Here you'll find three different challenges.[1] The instructions for the first, the *21-Day Challenge*, are set out here. So let's get started.

The 21-Day Challenge

I've heard it said that if you do something for twenty-one days, it's the start of a habit. Since reading your Bible is the best habit you can have, let's start here.

> **Lack of habit is the most common reason why people don't read the Bible more.**
>
> —Yankelovich marketing and advocacy study, January 13, 2006

The Gospel of John in the New Testament has twenty-one chapters. So for this challenge, you need to read one chapter of John every day for twenty-one days. Reading the chapter is the first step, but here are two more elements that will help you understand the Bible better. First, try reading each day with a pen and paper next to you and jot down the things that stick out to you about the passage. This will help you grasp what you're reading better. Second, each day after you are done reading, ask yourself these two questions: (1) What new thing did I learn from this chapter? and (2) How can I apply what I read to my life today?

---

[1] Resource information provided in this appendix may no longer be valid.

The 90-day (3-Month) Challenge

Read Genesis from the Old Testament as well as Matthew, Mark, and Luke from the New Testament.

The 6-Month Challenge

To take the *6-Month Challenge*, you'll read from Acts through Revelation in the New Testament as well as the Old Testament books of Psalms, Proverbs, and Ecclesiastes.

What can you do to call America back to the Bible? You can start with you. Come back to the only Book God ever wrote. Fill your life with his Word and watch him fill your life with his blessing.

Appendix
Two

Help Is On the Way

Nobody ever outgrows Scripture; the Book widens and deepens with our years.

—CHARLES HADDON SPURGEON

While the battle for Bible literacy continues, many have stepped forward to volunteer for God's army. In this appendix, we want to highlight some resources that may be useful to you in waging your own war against Bible illiteracy. Here you'll find annotated[1] Bible reading guides, Bible reading sites, books about how to read the Bible, online Bible studies, small-group resources, and a variety of other useful web sites and publications to combat Bible illiteracy. This list is by no means exhaustive. If you know of a web site, a book, or other resource that would make a welcome addition to this list, please forward your suggestion to www.bibleliteracycenter.com for future reference.

Bible Reading Web Sites[2]

- www.americanbibleorg. The site offers the text of the Greek New Testament right on the screen. This site is sponsored by the American Bible Society.
- www.backtothebible.org. The site provides five different Bible reading schedules (chronological, historical, Old and New Testament together, beginning to end, and blended) on screen

---

[1] Some of these annotations are taken from the publishers' descriptions of the books.
[2] As of this printing, the web sites in Appendix 2 are active.

and via AvantGo® downloadable to your handheld device. The site is sponsored by *Back to the Bible.*

- www.bible1.crosswalk.com. The site features the text of twenty-three Bible versions. The site is sponsored by Crosswalk.com.
- www.biblegateway.com. The site supplies the on-screen text of three Bible reading plans. The site is sponsored by BibleGateway.com.
- www.crusade.org. The Journey of Faith presents a reading schedule in the NIV text. The site is sponsored by Campus Crusade.

> **What's the best version of the Bible? The one you read.**
> —Woodrow Kroll

- www.dailybible.com. The site provides reading schedules and on-screen text in three English versions (CEV, KJV, TEV) and two Spanish versions. The site is sponsored by BibleNetUSA.
- www.heartlight.org. Five different Bible reading schedules. The site is sponsored by Heartlight.
- www.lifeway.com. Sponsored by Lifeway, this site features a daily reading schedule in pdf format.
- www.navpress.com. The site offers three downloadable Bible reading plans. The site is sponsored by NavPress.

Bible Reading Guides

Discipleship Journal's Book-at-a-Time Bible Reading Plan by Mark Bogart and Peter Mayberry (Colorado Springs, CO: NavPress, 2005).

Discipleship Journal's 5x5x5 Bible Reading Plan by Bill Mowry, Mark Bogart, and Peter Mayberry (Colorado Springs, CO: NavPress, 2005).

Back to the Bible's READ ME Bible Guides by Woodrow Kroll (Lincoln, NE: Back to the Bible, 2000). In one handy packet, you receive no less than seven different ways to read through the Bible in a year. Developed by *Back to the Bible's* international Bible teacher, the guides included are:

1) *Blended.* If you prefer not to read straight through the Bible but want to add variety to your Scripture reading, the blended approach is for you. While you are reading the Old Testament Book of Daniel, you are also reading the New Testament Book of Revelation; Leviticus is "paired" with Hebrews, etc.

2) *Chronological.* Read the events of the Bible as they occurred chronologically. For example, the book of Job is integrated with Genesis because Job lived before Abraham. Paul's epistles are strung through the record of Acts.

3) *Historical.* Read the books of the Bible as they occurred in the Hebrew and Greek traditions (the order in which they were written). For example, the Old Testament books in the Hebrew Bible do not occur in the same order as they do in our English Bible. The New Testament books are also arranged according to their date of writing.

4) *Morning and Evening.* As the name implies, this guide helps you read the Bible by beginning your day in the Old Testament and capping off that same day in the evening with a New Testament passage. This is for those of you who want to "book-end" your day with God's Word.

5) *Old and New Testament Together.* Read the Old and New Testaments together. Your knowledge of the Old Testament will be enhanced by what you read simultaneously in the New Testament.

6) *Start Anytime.* You don't have to wait until January 1 to begin reading your Bible. You can start anytime. With this guide you can read the Bible through in 365 days no matter when you begin.

7) *Weekend.* If your workdays are hectic and you claim you have insufficient time to read your Bible on workdays, this guide allows you to read through the entire Bible on weekends only—Saturday and Sunday. Set aside some time on those two weekend mornings, and you can read through the Bible in a year.

> The Bible is the most widely printed and distributed book of all time.
>
> —Woodrow Kroll

Online Bible Reading Guides May Be Found at:

- American Bible Society (www.americanbible.org)
- *Back to the Bible* (www.backtothebible.org)
- *Bible Reading Planner* (www.biblequizzes.com)
- *Daily Texts* (www.dailytext.com)
- National Bible Association (www.nationalbible.org)
- The Navigators (www.navigators.org)
- *Today's Bible Reading* (www.elca.org)

Audio Bible Reading Programs May Be Found at:

- *Back to the Bible* (www.backtothebible.org)
- Calvary Chapel Costa Mesa (www.MP3BiblePlayer.org)
- Faith Comes by Hearing, Hosanna, Albuquerque, New Mexico (www.faithcomesbyhearing.org)
- Faith Comes by Hearing, Canadian Bible Society (www.anglican.nb.ca)

Helpful Books on Reading the Bible

The Bible in 90 Days: Cover to Cover in 12 Pages a Day (Grand Rapids, MI: Zondervan, 2005).

The Bible in 90 Days Participant's Guide by Ted Cooper Jr. (Grand Rapids, MI: Zondervan, 2005). This curriculum is designed to assist those who choose to read through the Bible in ninety days. It helps you read the Scriptures as a story, enabling you to see that God's eternal purpose is unfolded continually and cohesively. The Participant's Guide gives brief overviews, provides study questions, and helps you keep going for the fourteen-week period of your reading.

Quiet Time Bible Guide: 365 Days through the New Testament and Psalms

by Cindy Bunch (Downers Grove, IL: InterVarsity, 2005). Dividing
the New Testament into 365 days of reading, the book offers you four
distinct approaches to each day: "Warming up to God," "Discovering
the Word," "Applying the Word," and "Responding in Prayer."

ESV One Year Bible (Wheaton, IL: Crossway, 2005).

How to Read the Bible Book by Book: A Guided Tour by Gordon D. Fee
and Douglas Stuart (Grand Rapids, MI: Zondervan, 2002).

How to Read the Bible for All Its Worth by Gordon D. Fee and Douglas
Stuart (Grand Rapids, MI: Zondervan, 2003).

*Footsteps through the Bible: A 52-Week Chronological Reading Plan and
Study Reference* by Richard M. Gagnon (Peabody, MA: Hendrickson,
2000).

How to Read the Bible So It Changes Your Life by Aletha Hinthorn (Kansas
City, MO: Beacon Hill Press, 2004).

Read Your Bible One Book at a Time by Woodrow Kroll (Ventura, CA:
Regal Books, 2004). If you picked up a bestseller by your favorite
author, you'd read the entire book, right? Do you think when Paul
wrote the Philippians he intended for them to read chapter one today,
chapter two tomorrow, and so on? Of course not. This was a letter;
they read it through in one sitting. Woodrow Kroll gives us sensible reasons why we should read each book of the Bible in single sittings.
Even more, he gives vital information about each book, what you
should look for in reading each book, and how much time it will take
you to read each book so you can read your Bible one book at a time.

> **Seventeen books of the New Testament contain less than
> ten chapters, and only two contain more than twenty-five
> chapters.**
>
> —Woodrow Kroll

How to Have a Quiet Time by Warren and Ruth Myers (Colorado Springs,
CO: NavPress, 1991).

NIV One-Year Bible (Carol Stream, IL: Tyndale, 1986).

The One-Year Chronological Bible NLT (Carol Stream, IL: Tyndale, 2000).

One Year through the Bible (Carol Stream, IL: Tyndale, 2000).

The MAP: Making the Bible Meaningful, Accessible, Practical by Nick Page
(Grand Rapids, MI: Zondervan, 2004).

Contemplative Bible Reading by Richard Peace (Colorado Springs, CO: NavPress, 1998).

Eat This Book by Eugene Peterson (Grand Rapids, MI: Eerdmans, 2006).

The Reese Chronological Bible edited by Edward Reese (Minneapolis, MN: Bethany, 1977).

> **69 percent of all Bibles purchased are bought as gifts.**
> —Crossway Books

How to Read the Bible as Literature by Leland Ryken (Grand Rapids, MI: Zondervan, 1984).

How to Read Your Bible by David Sanford and Renee Sanford (Nashville, TN: W Publishing Group, 2005).

The NIV Daily Bible: In Chronological Order by F. LaGard Smith (Eugene, OR: Harvest, 1999).

Knowing Scripture by R. C. Sproul (Downers Grove, IL: InterVarsity, 1977).

Reading through the Bible in One Year Made Easy by Mark Water (Peabody, MA: Hendrickson, 2003).

The Quiet Time Companion: A Daily Guide through the Bible by R. O. Willoughby, Colin Duries, and Alistair Hornal (Downers Grove, IL: InterVarsity, 2000).

Online Bible Studies

Bible.org. Offers various online text and video Bible studies (www.bible.org). Site sponsored by Bible.org.

BibleStudiesOnline.org. Offers various online Bible studies (www.backtothebible.org/biblestudies). Site sponsored by *Back to the Bible.*

Bible Study Planet. Site offers various online Bible studies (www.biblestudyplanet.com). Site sponsored by Bible Study Planet (Calvary Chapel Fellowship).

> **An April 2006 Pew study shows that 73 percent of Americans are Internet users, up from 66 percent in a similar study in January 2005.**
> —Pew Charitable Trusts

Gospel Communications. Clearing house for Bible studies online offered by Gospelcom.net clients (www.gospelcom.net/spiritual_walk/bible_studies). Site sponsored by Gospelcom.net.

Intervarsity Bible Studies. Site offers various online Bible studies (www.intervarsity.org/biblestu). Site sponsored by Intervarsity Christian Fellowship/USA.

Bible Study Programs: Adult

Augsburg Fortress Press offers an adult Bible studies program that covers the complete Bible during a six-year period. Web site: www.fortress-press.com.

Alpha. The Alpha course is a ten-week introduction to the Christian faith designed primarily for non-churchgoers and those who have recently become Christians. Web site: www.alphausa.org.

The Bethel Series. The Bethel Series uses the entire Bible to provide a framework for understanding the entire Bible. It is taught by lay people who have been trained by their ministers. Web site: www.bethelseries.com.

Bible Basics for Adults. This series includes inductive Bible study sessions in six series of ten lessons each. Offered by Augsburg Fortress. Web site: www.augsburgfortress.org.

The Bible Tutor. The Bible Tutor offers independent study and interactive self-testing. It is offered by Luther Seminary, St. Paul, Minnesota. Web site: www.luthersem.edu.

Crossways International. The Crossways ministry offers for adults and youth the big picture of the Bible, providing cultural and historical insights. Web site: www.crossways.org.

God's Word for Today series. The twenty-three volumes are produced and offered by Concordia Publishing. Web site: www.cph.org.

INSPIRE Bible Study Series. Produced by Augsburg Fortress, studies from Genesis to Revelation are offered. Web site: www.augsburgfortress.org.

Journeys Through God's Word Series. These courses are produced by Concordia Publishing and offer twelve sessions per volume. Web site: www.cph.org.

The Kerygma Program. The Kerygma Program offers a large variety of Bible studies for group or individual study. Web site: www.kerygma.net.

LifeLight Foundations. This new Bible study series provides a topical explo-
ration of the Bible. Produced by Concordia Publishing. Web site:
www.cph.org.

As you can see, I am passionate about you getting into God's
Word and staying there. Help is out there; you just have to choose
which resource is for you. I hope some of these resources will at
least get you started on your journey. The cost of losing the battle for
Bible literacy is too high to consider the possibility of that loss.
Still, Christians lose that battle daily, and God may use one of these
resources to help you win your own battle. If so, please write the
publisher of the book or resource and tell him what it was about
their product that was most helpful to you. You may be surprised
at how encouraging that will be to them.